The Voice of Our Congregation

SEEKING AND CELEBRATING GOD'S SONG FOR US

Terry W. York & C. David Bolin

Abingdon Press
Nashville

THE VOICE OF OUR CONGREGATION
SEEKING AND CELEBRATING GOD'S SONG FOR US

Copyright © 2005 by Abingdon Press

This book is printed on acid-free, recycled paper.

ISBN 0-687-34670-3

05 06 07 08 09 10 11 12 13 14 — 10 9 8 7 6 5 4 3 2 1

For
Janna and Julie

CONTENTS

PREFACE

E ach Sunday people drive past one or more local churches, which are closer to their home, to get to "their church." Often the by-passed churches include some of their own denomination, peopled, in part, by their friends and acquaintances. Why is that? What "voice" is calling them to one particular congregation? Constance Cherry suggests that "perhaps people in the new century don't need to find their worship style as much as they need to find their worship voice."[1]

Congregations have a voice; a corporate, unified voice, no matter how many opinions are expressed on any given issue. The voice has a message. It is the gospel and the truth that the gospel can be lived out in community. The voice has a mission. It is to whisper, shout, speak, and sing the message in daily conversation, times of need, and times of worship.

We are not the first to suggest that a congregation has a voice. For instance, in the spring of 1994, Garth Bolinder, pastor of Hillcrest Covenant Church in Prairie Village, Kansas, published a short, but intriguing article titled "Finding Your Worship Voice." In his article he wrote:

As any pastor knows, musical style is perhaps the biggest deal driving people's emotional response to worship. Many churches are a maelstrom of musical tastes, personality types, and worship preferences.

In an era of cultural diversity, how can one church find and develop its own authentic voice? With so many options available and so many individual preferences, how do we decide what will be our accent?[2]

It is the work of the congregation to find its voice, and, having found it, to continually refine that voice toward clarity and beauty in ministry and worship. The discovery of the voice need not be declared or defined. It will be intuited. The wise worship leader will detect and honor the voice.

The congregation sings an important song, yet its voice is more than an echo of the Master. The congregation's voice is the voice of testimony, praise, and prayer, rising from the lives and hearts of its individual members as a great congregational chorus that harmonizes by the grace, and in the Spirit, of God. The congregation's voice is often, if not *most* often, expressed in song. Finding songs that "fit" the congregation's voice is very closely associated with finding the voice itself. Their song must express their heart and soul. Their song must "fit," it must be authentic.

Unfortunately, a difficulty arises here. Rather than finding and singing their own song in their own voice, congregations all too often borrow or "import" songs from other congregations, other voices. It is tempting to borrow songs that seem "successful" in other congregational settings. It is tempting to import songs that are easier; songs that do not require us to search our soul. But those songs may be of another voice.

A congregation's songs may be difficult (not musically, but emotionally) as they express a particular sadness or spiritual challenge. Easy songs, especially easy songs borrowed from another voice, might fill a particular slot in the worship of the morning, but not express the heart, the true voice of the borrowing congregation. The borrowed songs, therefore, result in an imitating voice. These songs, at best, can only remain at the surface. Even the songs of joy a congregation sings must be the voice of their own joy. We cannot and need not borrow joy. In the first line of the gospel hymn, "He Keeps Me Singing" the singer confesses, "There's within my heart a melody."[3] This book exists to say to the congregations, "Sing *that* one. Whether or not it's in another congregation's repertory, sing it. Find your voice and use it to sing. Whether or not your songs have proved 'successful' in other settings, sing them."

How does a particular congregation find its voice? And having found it, how does the congregation know when to whisper, when to talk, when to shout, when to sing, even when to be silent?

This voice, and its wisdom, is found by listening to its overtones: the sympathetic vibrations set in motion by the congregation's love for God and for one another. It is the voice heard and shared when the congregation prays together, eats together, cries and rejoices together. It is the voice heard and shared when a congregation works out its differences, blesses its children, buries its saints, and sings its carols of love and hope. The voice of the congregation is heard when one sits alone in the sanctuary and remembers, or meets a member of the congregation out in the routine of daily life. It is a voice found first by listening, then by "joining in": in the singing, the praying, the fellowship. Having heard, recognized, and joined the voice (that is to say, added your voice into the grand chorus of the congregation), one carries the voice with them. In community, the individual members know, as one, when to whisper, talk, shout, sing, or be silent. In their hearts, in the soul of the congregation, they also know their common voice and its songs.

The voice of the congregation is the voice of two homes: home on this earth and home in heaven. People recognize the voice of home when they hear it. Jesus said, "My sheep hear my voice. I know them, and they follow me" (John 10:27). While that is true of the voice of the Good Shepherd, it is also true of the voice of the church, the congregation, the body of Christ (1 Cor. 12:27). The congregation is to do the work of Christ (be his hands and feet) and to speak his words (be his voice). The message of Christ, spoken and sung by the voice of the congregation, is the voice of past and future that calls us home in today's songs and stories.

The voice of the congregation is not limited to one genre or style. Its one message, one voice, and several emotions may well find expression in more than one type of song. The congregation will accept several styles as long as they are the songs of the one voice. A congregation's repertoire may well be similar to the repertoire of many other congregations. That's because the songs held in common speak of the *chorus* or *choir* of the larger family. Even so, each congregation will have its voice. The voice of the congregation will sing in harmony with the voice of the Spirit. The duet will be heard in the ears and hearts of all who will listen, even for a moment.

Listen for the still, small voice. Listen for the harmonizing voice of your congregation. Then sing, congregation, sing *your* song.

C. *David Bolin*
Terry W. York
Waco, Texas

Notes

1. Constance M. Cherry, "Merging Tradition and Innovation in the Life of the Church" in Todd E. Johnson, *The Conviction of Things Not Seen* (Grand Rapids, MI: Brazos Press, 2002), p. 32.

2. Garth Bolinder, "Finding Your Worship Voice," *Leadership: A Practical Journal for Church Leadership* XV:2 (Spring, 1994), pp. 26-33.

3. Luther B. Bridgers, "He Keeps Me Singing," *The Cokesbury Worship Hymnal* (Nashville: Abingdon Press, 1966), no. 110.

CHAPTER ONE

THE VOICE OF STARS AND STONES

"The morning stars sang together." (Job 38:7)

Before music—the sound of pipe or piano, the plaintive cello or forest drum, before the nightingale song or pounding surf on island shore—before it all, there came a Voice. With understated profundity, resolute authority, the Voice traveled through the darkness, across the surface of the waters to the deep places of the earth. That no ear could hear, or any voice answer, did not matter; the Voice was complete in and of itself.

"Let there be light."

And there *was* light.

Science says that light travels faster than sound. Even so, the Voice was first; it must come first. Without the Voice, there can be no light, no comprehension of what exists, and no imagination of what can be.

And the Voice continued to sound, awakening the earth from its slumber. The mountains rose and tossed their watery blanket aside to form great seas, luminous lakes, broad rivers, and cool running streams. The ground warmed to birth vegetation of all kinds—trees with tangy fruit and flowering plants of brilliant color. The tall grasses teemed with life—animals of every description, and palms stood as towering arches under the vaulted ceiling of the sky. In this, the most ancient and grandest of all cathedrals, the Voice thundered forth to call man from the dust of the ground, then woman from the rib of man. Here, also, the Voice came as a whisper visiting the two in the cool of the day. *Eden.* The name is synonymous with "paradise." The beauty of that pristine place cannot be told because no one has seen the earth in its unspoiled state. The most intuitive artist could never suppose to know all that was lost because of sin; and perhaps every work of art is in some way an attempt to gain entrance to the Garden.

The Voice called into being other voices. Just as the vibrations of one tuning fork will cause another fork to sound, creation responded in sympathetic vibration, joining in chorus with the foundational Word of God. The morning stars sang together; the trees of the field clapped their hands (Job 38:7; Isa. 55:12). Creation could do no less. This is why all things were made—to resonate to the Voice filling time and space with the glory of God.

> The heavens are telling the glory of God; and the firmament proclaims his handiwork. Day to day pours forth speech, and night to night declares knowledge. There is no speech, nor are there words; their voice is not heard; yet their voice goes out through all the earth, and their words to the end of the world. (Ps. 19:1-4)

Is the psalm simply the night imaginings of a boy shepherd? If so, then all biblical exhortations to actually sing and praise God for his handiwork could be dismissed as mere poetic expression. The congregation would have no voice, and there would be no reason for this book. Science, however, suggests that there is more. In a paper titled "Resonant Oscillations Between the Solid Earth and the Atmosphere," Japanese scientists have theorized as to the cause of a mysterious hum produced by the earth below the frequency of human hearing. Scientists have known about the hum for years but not its source. After analyzing seismic data, the Tokyo researchers postulated that sound waves in the lower atmosphere affect earth's surface to create sound waves inside the Earth. A similar phenomenon may occur on other planets, they noted, although the frequencies may be different.[1]

Does this research indicate that the morning stars literally do "sing" their Maker's praise? Though stars make sounds, we do not know that such is what God considers singing. Suffice it to say that creation does have a voice, and that each created entity responds to the Voice in its own way.

> Let the heavens be glad, and let the earth rejoice, and let them say among the nations, "The LORD is king!" Let the sea roar, and all that fills it; let the field exult, and everything in it. Then shall the trees of the forest sing for joy before the LORD, for he comes to judge the earth. (1 Chron. 16:31-33)

Man and woman were also given a voice by which they exercised dominion over creation. Unlike the morning stars, which could only respond to God with a word God had given, Adam and Eve were allowed to speak words of their own imagining. Like a parent who delights in hearing her child's first words, God enjoyed hearing what the man and woman would name the animals as God brought them one by one (or maybe two by two?). Adam and Eve delighted in hearing the voices God had bestowed on creation—the birdsong, the monkey's chatter, and the lion's roar. This enormous variety of sound, like Eden's variety of fruit, was made for their pleasure. Certainly too, the pair must have discovered their ability to imitate the sounds they heard, to sing high and low, loud and soft in phrases long and short. There was music as Adam and Eve, the first congregation, found their voice in the company of God.

We should not suppose, however, that the sounds in the Garden were the same as what can still be heard in nature. Eden was "paradise" in the aural as well as the visual sense of the word. Eve, for instance, was not surprised to hear the serpent speak, and the serpent's voice was beautiful, not the hissing sound associated with snakes. The sound, in fact, was so beguiling that for a moment Eve forgot the Voice and considered the serpent's lie. It promised that eating from the tree of the knowledge of good and evil would cause her and Adam to become like God; they would know what God knew; they could sing like the Voice sang. The artist recognizes the temptation and moment of turning to admire the luscious fruit of one's own creation—"my words, my thoughts, my feelings"—while forgetting the Voice that calls all things into being.

With a bite of forbidden fruit "their eyes were opened," and they saw themselves as they had not seen before. Their ears must also have been opened for they heard the Voice as they had not heard it before. The Voice they once gleefully ran to, now sent them running in terror. Furthermore their own voice was terribly altered; the song in the Garden that had been a duet of love became an aleatory counterpoint of contention—Adam accuses Eve, Eve accuses the serpent—the first split of a congregation.

Exiled from the sanctuary where they had worshiped God, Adam and Eve no longer ate from the tree of life. (Contentious congregations always end up banished from "life.") They could, however, continue to eat fruit from other trees, and though unable to hear the Voice of life, they continued, as well, to hear the voices of nature albeit in a fallen state. The birds still sang, the brook still murmured; still there was music. But no sound could ever fill the void left by the Voice, that awful voice Adam and Eve no longer wished to hear. Like today's rebellious teenagers, they had run into the bedroom, slammed the door, and turned the music of the world up full volume.

Without God's Voice, man and woman lost their command over the created order; the ground brought forth thorns and this-tles. Their loss was ever before them, and the Voice still stood at the door calling. But the door could not be opened without the Voice filling every corner of the room. So they said, "Let us make gods in our own image." Fashioned out of wood and stone, these gods didn't sing back, and musical incantations became, like idols, surrogates for the Voice. Examples of this are numerous through the Old Testament.

Dazzled by the Voice on the mountain, Moses descended to hear the noisy musical counterfeit that accompanied the worship of a golden calf.

> But he said, "It is not the sound made by victors, or the sound made by losers; it is the sound of revelers that I hear." As soon as he came near the camp and saw the calf and the dancing, Moses' anger burned hot, and he threw the tablets from his hands and broke them at the foot of the mountain. (Exod. 32:18-19)

Dancing on a stone altar, Baal's prophets called on their god to answer by fire. When the fire failed to fall, they screamed and cut themselves. "But there was no voice, no answer, and no response" (1 Kings 18:29).

An entertaining sideshow indeed, but the theatrics were no match for the fire that consumed Elijah's sacrifice. Humankind's problem has never been an inability to sing, scream, dance, or raise hands to heaven, but the failure to hear past its own voice the Voice of God. The prophet Isaiah listened, though, and the Voice spoke, saying:

> And he said, "Go and say to this people: 'Keep listening, but do not comprehend; keep looking, but do not understand.' Make the mind of this people dull, and stop their ears, and shut their eyes, so that they may not look with their eyes, and listen with their ears, and comprehend with their minds, and turn and be healed." (Isa. 6:9-10)

The Stones Will Cry Out

Through the centuries, Eastern Orthodox Christians have prayed "We see the most eloquent orators voiceless as fish concerning You, O Jesus our Savior" (*Akathist to Our Sweetest Lord Jesus*—Ikos 9). Whose voice *could* match his? The Gospel narratives observe that Jesus, unlike the religious rulers of his day, "taught as one having authority" (Matt. 7:29). To his followers, he was (and is) the very essence of the Law, and the fulfillment of the prophets' foretelling. He was the shepherd of Psalm 23 and the king of Psalm 24. His life was the embodiment of the testimony recorded in the sacred scrolls, read aloud in the synagogues, and treasured from generation to generation. Consider these two passages of scripture. The first passage is God's word through the prophet Isaiah.

> Ho, everyone who thirsts, come to the waters; and you that have no money, come, buy and eat! Come, buy wine and milk without money and without price. Why do you spend your money for that which is not bread, and your labor for that which does not satisfy? Listen carefully to me, and eat what is good, and delight yourselves in rich food. Incline your ear, and come to me; listen, so that you may live. (Isa. 55:1-3)

Jesus echoed these words when he cried to an assembly gathered in Jerusalem for the Festival of Tabernacles: "Let anyone who is thirsty come to me, and let the one who believes in me drink. As the scripture has said, 'Out of the believer's heart shall flow rivers of living water'" (John 7:37b-38).

Subtle? Not really, but just in case anyone failed to make this connection between scripture and himself, Jesus was even more direct: "You search the scriptures because you think that in them you have eternal life; and it is they that testify on my behalf. Yet you refuse to come to me to have life" (John 5:39-40).

His words sounded blasphemous, but they also sounded true. His words enlightened but confused; pardoned, yet condemned. People just couldn't figure Jesus out. Nicodemus called him "teacher"; the Samaritan woman called him "prophet." To the sick, he was a healer; to the hungry, he was the breadwinner; and to all, he was the greatest storyteller ever known. Once while praying with his disciples, Jesus suddenly asked, "Who do people say the Son of Man is?" Their response was varied. "Some say John the Baptist; others say Elijah; and still others, Jeremiah or one of the prophets." It's never easy to pigeonhole the truly one-of-a-kind. Unlike the prophet who merely resonated with the

Voice of God, in Christ could be heard the sound itself—the Voice that both silences and sets all other voices in motion.

> In the beginning was the Word, and the Word was with God, and the Word was God. He was in the beginning with God. All things came into being through him, and without him not one thing came into being. What has come into being in him was life, and the life was the light of all people. The light shines in the darkness, and the darkness did not overcome it.... And the Word became flesh and lived among us, and we have seen his glory, the glory as of a father's only son, full of grace and truth. (John 1:1-5, 14)

Among the apocryphal stories concerning the boy Jesus is one purportedly told by Matthew. On their flight to Egypt, Mary saw a palm tree and asked Joseph to collect its fruit while she sat with Jesus in its shade. Joseph, anxious to move on in search of water, balked at the thought of climbing a tree. The legend says that the child Jesus resting in his mother's arms said to the palm "O tree, bend thy branches, and refresh my mother with thy fruit."[2] Immediately, the tree bent down so its fruit could be taken and so remained until the child permitted it to again rise. The child spoke again saying, "Raise thyself, O palm tree, and be strong, and be the companion of my trees, which are in the paradise of my Father; and open from thy roots a vein of water which has been hid in the earth, and let the waters flow, so that we may be satisfied from thee."[3] The palm rose and yielded a cool spring to refresh the family and their beasts. The truth in the story is that with Jesus' birth, creation once again responded to the Voice. Water could become wine, a tree would wither and die, blind eyes could open, and a storm at sea become still. At the sound of the Voice, ocean waves would become a walkway, and the grave would surrender its captives.

As Jesus rode into Jerusalem on the back of a colt, the crowds waved palm branches and cheered, "Blessed is the king who comes in the name of the Lord! Peace in heaven, and glory in the highest heaven!" These words from Psalm 118 are those of a priestly blessing upon a procession of pilgrims. They adequately described the scene down to the waved palms, but now the worshipers rather than the priest spoke the words. Angered by this misuse, the Pharisees demanded that Jesus scold his disciples; but instead he rebuked them saying "I tell you, if these were silent, the stones would shout out." (Luke 19:40). With the rebuke, Jesus continues the language of Psalm 118, "The stone that the builders rejected has become the chief cornerstone" (Ps. 118:22). Was Jesus actually claiming that real stones would cry out and if so, how? The crucifixion suggests an answer.

> Then Jesus cried again with a loud voice and breathed his last.
> At that moment the curtain of the temple was torn in two,
> from top to bottom. The earth shook, and the rocks were split.
> (Matt. 27:50-51)

On the evening of November 8, 1914, an earthquake in the Santa Cruz Mountains of California was recorded for over four minutes by a seismograph. Some people heard the earthquake sounding like a low rumble and others as a "loud roar."[4] The sound from this comparatively mild earthquake would have been modest against the shock that tore Jerusalem's Temple curtain. In this sense, the stones did "cry out" as the Voice cried from the cross. Creation groaned while the congregation of disciples hid in silence (Rom. 8:22).

But let's go back and consider the possibility that Christ's reference to the psalm was only a metaphor to himself as the capstone. The apostle Peter made this same connection in his letter to the early church, describing Christ as the cornerstone and his followers as living stones.

> Come to him, a living stone, though rejected by mortals yet chosen and precious in God's sight, and like living stones, let yourselves be built into a spiritual house, to be a holy priesthood, to offer spiritual sacrifices acceptable to God through Jesus Christ. (1 Pet. 2:4-5)

In this light, Christ's rebuke shook the Pharisees with force stronger than an earthquake. Even if they were able to silence this rabble, the voice of praise would continue unabated as person after person, living stone after living stone, took its place. These stones constituted "a holy priesthood," and thus, the priestly blessing from the psalm was appropriately used. In Christ, the Word, the Voice, had become flesh and sounded again on earth. From stars to stones, the Word of God would again resonate through all creation and find its greatest sounding board in the voice of the "holy priesthood"—the congregation.

Singing with Stars and Stones

The congregation's voice fills the sanctuary following a service as the organ plays and the members greet one another in friendship and love. Meander through the crowd, do a little eavesdropping, and you will hear snippets of conversation accounting the joys and concerns of the people who worship in this place. If, however, you wish to know this congregation's heart, listen to their voices joined in song. What songs do they sing? How are they accompanied? Do the people fervently sing the familiar words? Do they wrestle to master new ones? The congregation's singing tells you who they are.

Many factors will have influenced the music you hear—theology, tradition, ecclesiology, the birth years of the membership, and even the acoustics of the room. As the relative strengths of harmonics and partials determine the timbre of a musical instrument, these factors determine the sound of the congregation's voice. To say each congregation is unique is as trite a phrase as "no two snowflakes are alike," or so it would seem. Why, then, do so many congregations buy into the marketing myth that to reach the world for Christ, they must abandon their uniqueness to adopt *the* model (and music) that "speaks" to contemporary culture (as though culture was monolithic as well)?

In Matthew's account of the triumphal entry into Jerusalem, Jesus quotes a passage from Psalm 8.

But when the chief priests and the scribes saw the amazing things that he did, and heard the children crying out in the temple, "Hosanna to the Son of David," they became angry and said to him, "Do you hear what these are saying?" Jesus said to them, "Yes; have you never read, 'Out of the mouths of infants and nursing babies you have prepared praise for yourself'?" (Matt. 21:15-16)

At birth, the child greets the world with a victory cry marking the completion of nine months in the womb. The cry is evidence that the lungs and vocal cords have developed as they should. It will be heard many times in the months to come—on one occasion announcing hunger, or on another the need for a diaper change. Every cry is an acknowledgment that someone, parent or guardian, is bigger and able to provide for the child's need. This uninhibited exercise of the voice is not an acquired skill but something God has "prepared," just as God made stars to sing. Like the unborn child, each congregation's voice is being fashioned by God. In the womb of experience, the voice develops through victory and trial, through the coming and going of its members with their tastes, understandings, abilities, and energies. Every worship service is an act of birth and every song is the congregation's birth cry sounding forth the praise God has "prepared." The voice is no accident; it is a work of creation.

The prophet Ezekiel heard the Voice and described it as follows: "the sound was like the sound of mighty waters; and the earth shone with his glory" (Ezek. 43:2). The apostle John heard the same magnificent sound in his heavenly vision on the isle of Patmos: "And I heard a voice from heaven like the sound of many waters and like the sound of loud thunder; the voice I heard was like the sound of harpists playing on their harps" (Rev. 14:2).

Tour groups cluster to sing at Jerusalem's Garden Tomb. Stand between the clusters and you will hear the voice "of many waters" as different languages and musical styles converge in the sound of praise. If you can imagine what angels hear as songs of adoration the world over ascend to heaven on a Sunday morning, you may sense how deep and wide is the voice "of many waters." The oboe need not sound like the clarinet, or the clarinet as the trumpet. Each instrument has its part to play. So too, each congregation has been given its own unique timbre for a symphony of praise. In this orchestration of many voices, God recreates a musical paradise rivaling the sounds of Eden itself.

When your congregation gathers in its place of worship, the Voice also comes to sing along. Never rude, God calls—waiting to hear the congregation answer with the voice God has made. "Listen! I am standing at the door, knocking; if you hear my voice and open the door, I will come in to you and eat with you, and you with me" (Rev. 3:20).

The eighteenth-century English hymn writer William Cowper understood that "Sometimes a light surprises the child of God who sings; it is the Lord who rises with healing in his wings."[5] Perhaps we are only "sometimes" surprised because only sometimes do we listen for the Voice that calls at the door. Perhaps we only "sometimes" see the light because our arguments on musical efficacy and appropriateness are the bushel that covers the light, keeping us in the darkness. We debate over which musical fruit to eat and never eat from the Tree of Life. As a consequence, we join Adam and Eve banished from the Garden where the Voice of Life sings.

Every congregation confronts the choice—to make noise or music, to scream like the prophets of Baal or resonate to the foundational Voice of God. A congregation can attempt to remake its voice in culture's image or sound forth its God-given uniqueness, joining stars and stones in the symphony of praise. The choice would seem easy, but it never is. For this reason, there is much for us to consider in the pages ahead.

Notes

1. Roy Britt, "Source of Earth's Hum Revealed, Space Symphony Possible," March 26, 2000 (http://www.space.com/scienceastronomy).

2. Writings of the Anti-Nicene Fathers, vol. VIII, "The Gospel of Pseudo Matthew" (http://www.ccel.org/fathers2/ANF-08/anf08-68 .htm#LOC_P5970_1750772).

3. Ibid.

4. Carl H. Beal, "Earthquake in the Santa Cruz Mountains, California, November 8, 1914," Bulletin of the Seismological Society of America, Vol. 4, pp. 215-19.

5. William Cowper, "Sometimes a Light Surprises" in *The Covenant Hymnal: A Worshipbook* (Chicago: Covenant Publications, 1996), no. 94.

CHAPTER TWO

THE VOICE OF POETS AND PROPHETS

But Jesus said to them, "Prophets are not without honor except in their own country and in their own house." (Matt. 13:57b)

In his remarkable book, *Finally Comes the Poet,* Old Testament scholar Walter Brueggemann writes, "Those whom the ancient Israelites called prophets, the equally ancient Greeks called poets. The poet/prophet is a voice that shatters settled reality and evokes new possibility in the listening assembly."[1] Isn't that why you are reading this book? You want to "shatter settled reality and evoke new possibility" in your worship and its music, but you want to do so without shattering the community in the process and you want the "new possibility" to be authentic in the context of your congregation.

God places poet/prophets in every congregation. God speaks through these persons or groups of people when God chooses to do so. The beauty of it is that it is not always the same person or group on every issue. Therefore, one of the tasks or responsibilities of the congregation is to develop a reliable sense of discernment. Discernment requires great humility on the part of everyone in the congregation, clergy and laity alike. We are not good at humility. It is easier to import music and worship styles than to discover and develop our own authentic expressions. Further, we can trust God's voice to always be right, but we cannot always trust God's will and promptings to be expedient. We cannot trust God to sign on to our agendas and schedules. God is not in our employ. We are to serve God and one another. Therefore, humility before one another and before God is absolutely necessary if the voice of God is to be heard in the voice of the congregation. Interestingly, courage is needed as well; courage to speak, courage to listen, courage to act. But remember, *humility* and courage are more closely related than are *brashness* and courage.

The very words *poet* and *prophet* speak of this strange combination of humility and courage. They also speak of timelessness and strength. The words suggest truth and wisdom that is God-spoken through the poet/prophet's speaking or writing. But, they also evoke visions of unusual people; hermits or strange, out-of-touch misfits. That is an understandable, but unfortunate stereotype. It is an important breakthrough in our understanding of how the Holy Spirit works in a local congregation when we come to realize that there are poets and prophets in our midst. They are not "angels unawares"; they are familiar folks whom we know to be dedicated to God and the congregation. They can be trusted.

It is good for us to remember that rhyme can be bent to serve our lies and oratory can be bent to serve a shady agenda, but poetry and prophecy speak the truth and resist manipulation. Respected members of the congregation (truly respected, not just the loudest or those with the highest profile) do not bend and manipulate. They speak truth and resist manipulating or being manipulated.

The congregation does not elect poets and prophets. They are not, necessarily, to be found up front on Sunday morning. Look for them out among the congregation. Often, there are several in a congregation and they seem to be able to articulate what the congregation is thinking at a deep level. The very fact that these people exist and function in this way is evidence that a congregation is an entity with a voice and that the voice is clearly present in these persons, even if they represent the "minority report." The voice is recognizable at a deep level within the congregation and is unique to that congregation. In a real sense, finding the voice of the congregation is finding God's voice in the congregation. This realization does not diminish the prophetic role of the pastor or others on the ministerial staff. But it does speak to the fact that God can and does speak through individuals in the community of worshipers as much as God speaks through those who lead in worship. The role of the pastor includes helping his or her congregation understand the power of the Holy Spirit at work in their midst; the power, the call, and the resulting voice.

Finding the Voice

There is great wisdom in a group of people called together by the Holy Spirit and bound together by their brotherhood and sisterhood in Christ. It simply stands to reason that a community of Christ-followers with this kind of congregational awareness would also have its own voice for worship. Some songs and worship styles will fit this voice and some won't. That's true of any voice. Authenticity is the dynamic here. New songs can be brought into this repertoire, but only if they speak the truth and sound it forth in the authentic voice. Something that is fake or pretend is not only apparent to God, it is apparent to all who hear it. Even the singer knows such a song and the singing of it to be shallow. The poets and the prophets in a congregation will sense whether or not the song, old or new, can authentically come from this voice. Don't assume that all resistance is stubbornness or ignorance. Resistance may simply be the "INAUTHENTIC" alarm going off.

It must be said here, of course, that not all of the angry, vocal people who push back against change represent the voice of God in our midst. Again, discernment is important. Communal discernment becomes more reliable as an increasing number of people in the congregation come to understand the concept of a congregational voice. This voice can be heard in much the same way an individual can hear their heartbeat: through quiet concentration on the internal. The "still, small voice" is not a fairy tale. God the Holy Spirit is real, but does not shout, personally or congregationally.

What does it mean when we say that a writer or a performer has finally "found their voice"? It means that there has finally emerged from within them an authenticity that makes their performance, their work, their contribution something new and of value, indeed, a *contribution*, no longer simply imitation. Who they are begins to shine through their technical skill. We cannot borrow music or art of any form from someone else and claim it is ours or expect it to speak of our soul unless it connects with who we are and can authentically be expressed by our voice. This is especially true in our worship of God. We give back to God what God has given us. This gift will be unique in its combination of what God has given us and what we (not someone else) have done with it. Why is it that we can stand before one painting and "feel" nothing and then move down the wall a few feet, stand in front of another painting and suddenly realize we are weeping? Both paintings may be by recognized masters. Both may be priceless. But one may not connect with who we are. When that is the case, it does not call to our voice, thus our voice does not respond.

Possession of the Voice

The congregation possesses a common or communal voice that is the sound of God in their midst. The voice possesses the congregation. God is in them and around them. Authentic worship, worship that is initiated by the voice of God and is expressed in the voice of the congregation, worship that pulls us heavenward, is not bigger than life; it is as deep as life. It must, of course, be that particular congregation's life. The poets and prophets among us won't let us forget that fact.

Poets and prophets often operate outside prescribed rules and popular trends. Every congregation has those members who, whether or not they are formally elected to places of leadership, are acknowledged as leaders who have the right to challenge popular impulses. That is an example of being aware, even subconsciously, that God's voice does not sound from the pulpit only, that God isn't restricted to our organizational charts and agendas. It is an example of what some traditions refer to as the priesthood of the believer. So, if the congregation is a voluntary gathering of priests, each with the capacity of speaking God's words, it stands to reason that that group would have a common (do not read "unison") voice. That voice is best expressed in songs (monophonic and polyphonic) that reflect its message, mission, and heart. The congregation may know a song the minister of music or worship leader doesn't know. Such a song is a treasure that they are not going to treat recklessly. They will not shout it above the songs selected for Sunday, but they will measure Sunday's songs against the treasured repertoire. The wise and caring minister will seek to learn the congregation's song(s) through the mining process of personal relationships and listening. At that point, the minister of music has "permission" to introduce new songs that, because they fit the voice of the congregation, will come to be treasured by them.

I was given some valuable advice years ago when I was considering taking a ministerial position in a church in Hawaii. A man in the inviting congregation told me that if I decided to accept the position, I should not change anything until I had learned to surf. As it turned out, I did not feel led to accept that position, but I have never forgotten the advice. He was telling me to be vulnerable, to "learn" the world and way of the congregation. He was telling me to take the time required to discern the voice of that particular congregation. When one has "learned to surf," any changes made will be in the context of that culture. The changes will be informed and cloaked in love. We will not come from our "mainland" to their "island" and attempt to make them like us. There is a voice and it is deep and quiet. It was humming before any of us arrived on the scene and it will be humming when we leave. Listen to the poets and prophets who express the voice most naturally, with a sense of reverence and respect for it.

I once became the associate pastor of a large congregation. Much of the day-to-day operation of the congregation's life and ministry was covered by my job description. It would be almost impossible to get to know everyone in that large community, but I needed to know the congregation's voice in order to fulfill my responsibilities properly. Though I wasn't the minister of music, I needed to know this particular community's "songs." I began my "voice lessons" by finding out who was the oldest living charter member of the fifty-year-old congregation. Her name was Mrs. Davis. I called up one of her sons and asked if I could take his mother to lunch. I was delighted that he not only said "yes," but that he offered to come along.

At lunch I asked Mrs. Davis a simple, but important question, "Mrs. Davis, what do I need to know about this church?" She talked more than she ate. I ate and listened. She and her son beamed as she related chapter after chapter of the congregation's story. I was hearing the story and beginning to discern the story's soundtrack; to recognize its song and its voice. She knew the poetry of it all; the little things that were important for me to know because they pointed to the big things for which I now had some responsibility. Her voice nearly sang as her eyes glistened. The word got out that I had had lunch with Mrs. Davis and that she did all the talking. The word got out that I wanted to know who these people were and what story I had been invited into, that I was purposefully tuning my ear to hear the voice of the congregation. Though we didn't use the exact words, the congregation knew that I knew they had a voice, a story, a song.

There were other similar lunches, but far beyond lunches, bits and pieces of the story were being offered to me as welcoming gifts; gifts from the congregation's poets and prophets, their wise men and women, the ones to whom the congregation listened for the final and practical word of God in that setting. I felt a qualified permission to lead. I had been educated—not programmed, not handcuffed, but appropriately educated. Preach, if you will, from what you know. Sing if you will, from what you know. That is why they have called you here, but if your words are to be effective, they must harmonize with the voice of the congregation.

The voice that we begin to discern in the congregation is a voice that has been tuned by years spent in the Bible, the hymnal, and the trenches. The words of the poets and prophets from across the ages have been sought out, heeded, taught, and sung in the midst of this congregation. Opinions and agendas have been allowed to roam freely in this arena, but the arena has parameters. God's word through God's poets and prophets (biblical and congregational), have set the parameters, giving focus, guidance, and an authoritative voice over the years. We learn through the biblical accounts *and* we learn through the life-testimonies of the poets and prophets around us, who live their interpretations of the scripture, that the voice of the congregation and its biblical song possess us as much as we possess them. We know when our ventures into new music and new worship styles have moved us beyond our authentic voice. We feel it in our bones, in our hearts. We often hear the admonition to congregations to move out of their comfort zone. That is a legitimate challenge because the voice of the congregation may well be a wider circle than the current circumference of their comfort zone. But we must never ask a congregation to move beyond the authentic expression that is their voice. Seldom do we hear a congregation say "no new songs." More often we hear "not *those* new songs." We must listen. We must lead. We must move forward. But we must not do so in disharmony with the voice of the congregation.

One of the characteristics of poets and prophets is that they are possessed by the message. When they hear God's voice they can heed no other. We encountered this concept earlier. Let's look a bit closer at it here. When a congregation hears God's voice calling them back or forward to their authentic voice, some will choose to ignore the call. It is the poet/prophet(s) who will speak up against such ignorance (read that word carefully). The voice of the poets and prophets will remind the congregation of their voice and its responsibility to sound forth in subservience to God's voice. God possesses the congregation, individually and corporately. We are the Shepherd's sheep. The congregation does not possess its God. The voice of the congregation is obligated to say "yes" to the voice of God. The voice of God is still and small, but it exists in the hearts and heart of the congregation. We cannot escape it. We can ignore it and sing someone else's song, but we will be aware of the insincerity of such a song.

Finding the voice of the congregation is submitting our will to God's will, our way to the Shepherd's way. The song possesses us; we do not possess the song. We may want to sing higher, lower, faster, slower, newer, older, but "not my will, but thine be done" is our model.

Finding the voice of the congregation isn't just about music, just as worship isn't just about music. Finding the voice of the congregation is about bowing to God's will, loving God more than we love ourselves, and using the talents God gave us instead of acting as if we have the talents God gave someone else. To worship, work, and witness in the authentic voice of the congregation is to be a humble and grateful servant working with what we have been given in the field to which we have been sent. We are up to something questionable when we disguise our voice. We are trying to get out from under the requirements and responsibilities of who we are when we disguise our voice. For a moment we want to be someone else, so we hide the evidence that identifies us until the charade is over. To use our voice is to admit to who we are. That's true for individuals and for congregations. Are we not to worship in spirit and in truth? (John 4:23). Listen to the poets and the prophets in your congregation, be they few or many. The poet/prophet always calls us to speak, sing, and live the truth, back onto the path, forward on the Way. The song that is sung authentically from the voice of the congregation owns us. We do not own it.

Giftedness and the Voice

Particular giftedness is a strong indication that God has a unique voice in mind for each congregation's worship and proclamation. Imagine the folly of God gifting congregations A, B, and C differently and then expecting congregations B and C to strive to be like congregation A. God wants us to worship God, not them.

Particular giftedness also suggests that everyone in the congregation is to contribute to worship and proclamation as poet/prophet (Rom. 12:4-8). The gospel message is always the same, though the mode of proclamation and application (giftedness) may well differ from poet to poet, prophet to prophet, congregation to congregation. Poets are to write the words given to them. They are not to envy (though they may admire) the work of other poets. Prophets are to speak the words given to them. They are not to envy (though they may admire) the "success" of other prophets. It's the same for congregations. It is a breakthrough moment when a congregation decides to look within rather than "go shopping" when the time comes to consider what their music and worship style should be. The answer to what music and worship style a congregation should employ is to be found within its own giftedness. God provides what we need to do the tasks to which we are called. "God, I don't want to do what you've gifted me to do, I want to do what you gifted him/her to do." What is your reaction to the preceding sentence? Your reaction may be similar to God's reaction when your congregation decides it wants to be like another congregation. Pause here a moment and think about this. Such a statement is like a prophet saying, "I don't want to say that," or "I don't want to say that to those people." Read, again, the book of Jonah, especially the early verses of chapter 4.

We cease to be the prophet/poets we are meant to be when we get the idea that giftedness and worship is for us or about us. We have focused totally on ourselves when we are disappointed with our gifts and envious of others' gifts, when what *they* "get to do" seems more fun or more successful that what *we* "get to do." We are God's children, but that does not give us permission to be childish. Coming to grips with who we are is a sign of maturity that is absolutely necessary if we are to live authentic lives. That is true for congregations as well as for individuals. A congregation must find and speak/sing/worship in its own voice. Saying "yes" to God is saying "yes" to our giftedness, for we are gifted to accomplish the tasks God gives us.

The poets and prophets in our midst do not always call us *back* to our authentic voice. Sometimes they call us *forward* to our authentic voice. Either way, it is a call to a continuing deepening of our Christ-following and discipleship. Too often, congregations would rather try to be like another congregation than explore the depths of their own giftedness and mission. The poets and prophets in the congregation sense when this is happening and speak up to expose it, whether the call is back to authenticity or forward to authenticity. When the entire congregation realizes the direction toward authenticity and moves, as one, in that direction, the congregation has accepted the "call to Nineveh." When that happens, God is not only worshiped authentically on Sunday, but also throughout the week as the congregation goes about the mission of being church and living the gospel daily. There is no more duality in their living. It is always authentic and always toward Christlikeness. It is important for us to know and own our true identity, our true giftedness.

The Pastor and the Voice

Earlier in this chapter we stated that the role of the pastor includes helping his or her congregation understand the power of the Holy Spirit at work in their midst; the power, the call, and the resulting voice. The clergy must help the laity embody the voice of the congregation. In other words, the shepherd must call forth the poet/prophet that exists in the soul and giftedness of each member of the congregation and in the soul and giftedness of the congregation as a whole. Perhaps the simple word here is "involvement," but it is a level of involvement that requires commitment to spiritual growth as a Christian and a congregation. This has been called by several names over the years and across denominations. Some of the more common names are *discipleship* and *equipping the saints*. We cannot forget or ignore the fact, however, that congregational self-discovery involves more than skill training. It has to do with a spiritual understanding of the life and work of the worshiping community.

It is a sad thing to see a congregation shirk its responsibility to God by allowing pastoral dictatorship in the guise of honoring the authority of the office of pastor. That congregation will be more susceptible than others to shirking its responsibility to God by mimicking other congregations' music and worship patterns. We are not to delegate to others the responsibilities that are specifically ours. Pastors must continually give "the story" back to the people, including the story's responsibilities. "The story," from the big end to the little end, is the story of God's work throughout history, the gospel of Jesus Christ, the history of the church, the history of your particular congregation and the Holy Spirit at work in the individual. In other words, the pastor is to constantly remind his or her flock that the voice of God the Father, speaking through God the Son and God the Holy Spirit, finally results in God's speaking to and through individuals in community as the voice of the congregation. The congregation must not seek to alter that sacred voice through imitation of another or deferring to another. The pastor must remind the people, as often and in as many ways as necessary, to allow God's voice, and God's alone, to speak to their hearts and through their actions; to be the poet/prophet God wants them to be. But it is quite tempting for congregation and pastor, alike, to opt for the easier, more "efficient" voice placed solely in the pastor. Placing the voice and its responsibilities there feeds egos and releases responsibility. In such a situation, the pastor's one voice is declared to be the congregation's unison voice. If the pastor is not a musician (which, by the way is neither a sin nor a character flaw) and has been allowed to be the sole voice in and for the congregation, he or she might be tempted to adopt an "outside" voice for the congregation's music and worship. It would be a quick and easy "fix" of an important item on the pastor's overwhelming "to do" list.

When the pastor is honored, not as the only poet/prophet, but as first among peer poets and prophets, the congregation will be more likely to be aware of their communal voice and less likely to forsake that voice. The voice may not always sound forth in unison, but it will sound forth harmoniously. *These words are not a scolding of the pastor or of the congregation.* They are a call to all of us to own and honor what we know about our congregation at a spiritual level. It is a call to move forward in our worship and its music, but to do so authentically; to do so with the understanding that to move forward will likely mean going deeper into who we are as a congregation.

Creativity and the Voice

We must not assume that the voice of the congregation will inevitably grow old and out of touch. New people are being born into the congregation on a regular basis, both physically and spiritually. There is a freshness there, a spring of life.

"But," you may be asking, "what about congregations that seldom experience either source (physical or spiritual) of new energy and ideas?" How is their voice to remain creative and vital? Let us remind ourselves of the title of this chapter, "The Voice of Poets and Prophets." In a congregation like this, sometimes the best the poet/prophet can do is to simply lead the rest of the congregation to listen and to be aware. This is what poets do. This is how poets "hear" what they are to write. They listen closely to conversations and to God in the silent part of prayer when they have said all of their words. They listen to the Holy Spirit speak through the scripture. They watch, too. They watch for a glimmer, however slight, a glimmer of hope or a glimmer of an answer. Sometimes what they are compelled to write or speak is unwelcome or difficult to accept. Yet, they know it to be truth, and those who hear and read recognize its truth. Poets don't get their poems from crystal balls. They get their poems from everyday events and conversations and surroundings. In fact, they do their best work when they "mine" the mundane, routine, even hopeless realities of life and find there a poem, a prophecy of hope. The poet/prophet forces us to look at the truth. God is truth. God helps us move forward toward God's ultimate truth. The spark of God's presence is present in every Christian's heart, thus in every congregation, no matter how obscured it may have become over the years. The poet/prophet(s) within the congregation will be able to point to God's presence, to fan the spark(s) into flame. What is being said here can be dismissed as just so much ethereal, misty, philosophical, psychobabble. Or, you can pause in silence, listen to the Holy Spirit whisper in your heart, and know it to be true, if somewhat buried, even in your situation. Take heart. God knows how to create and to resurrect. Let's return to the voice of the congregation and creativity.

When we open ourselves to being creative, we must watch that we don't slip over into gimmickry. A general rule of thumb (not 100 percent reliable) is that creativity comes from within and gimmickry comes from without. When we venture toward something new we seem to know intuitively whether or not it is creative or simply a gimmick. Our worship must always be free of gimmicks. Again, in general terms, if you are wondering if the new idea is a gimmick or not, it probably is. Creativity has an air of honesty about it, the authenticity we've been discussing. The congregation will warm up to authentic creativity, but will turn a cold shoulder to gimmickry. They will instinctively know if the "new song" can be sung in the voice of the congregation or if they are going to have to pretend. This is why major or long-term change is best approached in small increments. Each authentic increment emboldens the congregation toward the next. They need time to understand and test the new idea, step by step. Before they know it, they are on an authentic journey into creativity in their music and worship. They will realize that they have found the voice of the congregation and will become confident and comfortable in using it to sing new songs.

Poet/prophets as leaders point the way. Poet/prophets as followers recognize the truth or rightness of the path. In both roles, creativity becomes a welcome and familiar conversation companion of those who watch, listen, speak, and move in the secure freedom of poetry. Poetry is often more appropriate than prose when the created is trying to worship the Creator. We should expect the Creator's instruction, leadership, and urgings to be creative. How could it be otherwise? Further, the Creator is not going to lead us in a false or unauthentic manner. Creativity that will enhance our worship and will be true to the voice of our congregation will come from within or will be able to be authentically adopted if imported from brothers and sisters of another congregation. Finding the voice of your congregation isn't an exercise in isolationism. We can and should learn from other believers. They are a source of creativity. But we must accept the fact that while new songs and methods of worship can be forced on a congregation, authenticity cannot. Poet/prophets cannot help but speak against imported worship that lacks authenticity.

Two African American congregations come to mind: the first, a Baptist congregation in California, the second, an AME congregation in Texas. A friend of mine, a fellow college student who was a member of the congregation, invited me to worship with the California congregation. The service began with about eight older men moving from their front row seats to stand in a line, facing the congregation. After one of these deacons had led in a prayer that was as much sung as it was said, backed by beautifully intoned encouragement from the rest of the men in the line, the same man began leading the congregation in one of the most fascinating forms of hymn singing I had ever experienced. I now know it was "lining-out," also referred to as "deaconing" or "Dr. Watts." I had never heard anything so alive with emotion and meaning, so enriched by its obvious links to the old call-and-response form of antebellum field songs. I was moved as a musician, a budding music history/hymnology student, as a Christian, and as a worshiper. It was perhaps the most heart-gripping worship experience of my life at that point. As we left the worship service, my friend asked what I thought about what had taken place. He knew this was a first for me. As I began to talk about the lining-out, he interrupted me. He was apologizing that I had had to sit through that "old stuff," which he and others of his age in the congregation hoped would soon fade away. He was an advocate for new music experiences in his congregation's worship. In the conversation that ensued he was able to see his familiar worship experience through my "new eyes." He saw how *the story*, the congregation's story, and his story were "present" in the worship. He did not give up on his hope for a refreshing of worship in that setting, but he was now able to see that change had to take place in and show respect for that setting, those worshipers, and the voice of that congregation.

In the second instance, the AME congregation in Texas, there was no "deaconing" as such. However, I visited on a Sunday when it was the deacons' turn to provide the music leadership in worship. They processed in with stately, seasoned voices, moving down the center aisle. They stopped at the front of the sanctuary, knelt, and led in prayer. After the prayer, they continued their singing processional up into the choir loft. The congregation sang along, young people and older people alike. This was the deacons' Sunday. The youth would have theirs, the women theirs, and others as rotation and congregational involvement dictated. Here the congregation seemed to be very much in touch with their voice. It sounded forth in harmony and a deep sense of community. In both instances I saw what seemed to me to be authentic creativity. True, in both congregations the events I saw for the first time were very familiar to them. But that familiarity does not negate the creativity. Creativity does not mean something new every Sunday. Creativity means that what is happening continues to be meaningful, continues to communicate *the story*, and continues to enliven the voice of the congregation. The new will show up from time to time, but will always find its meaning in its connection to the old, the established, the voice. In healthy congregations worship will always be open to evolving and developing. But the evolving and developing will not be willy-nilly or haphazard. It will always be in the context of the voice of the congregation. If not, the new things will serve only to destroy one congregation and start another in the same pews, over and over again. That is not healthy reform. It is shortsighted rejection. The voice of the poet/prophets will blend in with what is happening when the voice of the congregation is being honored, even in times of change. However, the voice of the poet/prophet will sound shrill against what is happening when the voice of the congregation is being ignored.

Culture and the Voice

Jesus' prayer for his disciples in John 17 is one of the most poignant passages in all of scripture. In this prayer, Jesus expresses his concern about our struggles with "the world" after he is crucified, buried, resurrected, and ascends back into heaven. He knew that sending us into the world to teach what we have been taught and to baptize in his name would make us vulnerable to the world's influences. It's a two-pronged vulnerability. We are not only susceptible to the world's influence in times of weakness, but also in the times of our strongest dedication to our mission, as the voice of the congregation strives to proclaim God's message in the world's language. The dynamic tension is tense, indeed. Jesus prayed, "I have given them your word, and the world has hated them because they do no belong to the world, just as I do not belong to the world. I am not asking you to take them out of the world, but I ask you to protect them from the evil one. They do not belong to the world, just as I do not belong to the world" (John 17:14-16). We do not spend enough time with this passage of scripture.

We should read Jesus' prayer every time we are about to allow the culture to tell us how to worship. Jesus does not belong to the world and neither do we. We are to overhear this prayer as instruction to us. "The community must not lose sight of the reality that its own life and proper identity are a gift from God.... The prayer, therefore, orients believers towards God and invites them to find in God insight into their own identity." [2]

One's voice is a big part of one's identity; so, too, a congregation's identity. We must ask ourselves if our intense desire to have our worship relate to the culture around us is motivated by the hope that if our worship does relate corporately to the unredeemed culture, we, as individuals, won't have to. Perhaps the thinking is somewhat the opposite: if our worship tunes its voice to the culture around us, it will be easier for us to represent our congregation while we are scattered during the week. Both possibilities point to the temptation to use worship to protect us from the peculiarity of the "not belonging" that we are called to. Any one teenage or older adult knows the fear and/or the pain of not being accepted by the crowd, of being different. Yet, Jesus has made it clear that neither he (the One being worshiped) nor we (the worshipers) belong to the world. We are not to abandon the voice of the congregation in favor of or even for the sake of the voice of the world around us.

Surrounded by this kingdom's culture while proclaiming the kingdom of heaven's message, the congregation must stay close to God's poets and prophets—those in scripture, behind the pulpit, and in the pews. The voice of the congregation must speak with the accent of heaven so that those with whom we speak will be able to detect the fact that we are citizens of some other place.

If we learned anything in the worship wars, it was that camouflaging our worship, so that we might infiltrate the surrounding culture, leads to chaos, mistaken identities, and "friendly fire." The gospel infiltrates the surrounding culture through the unmasked, unusual, radical love of Christ apparent in those who claim to be Christ-followers. The voice of the congregation must speak that love to and among the surrounding culture in a voice so unique, authentic, and unified in harmony that it turns heads: "What was that? It sounded like nothing I've ever heard before. I've never heard anything like that around here." These quotes comes in two varieties: ridicule and inquiry. We don't get to choose. The more we disguise our voice to avoid ridicule or to be "effective," the less the voice elicits inquiry. The voice of the congregation is called upon to simply speak the truth and worship in truth, requiring both, of course, to be authentic.

The culture will have its influence on the congregation and their worship. It cannot and should not be avoided. Neither should the surrounding culture dictate our worship style/music to us or be given the power of veto. Having said that, we acknowledge that the people in the sanctuary for an hour or two on Sundays have spent far more time in "the world" Monday through Saturday. They will track in some of the "mud." That's okay. But our being in the world and not of it should result in worship that affects our culture more than culture that affects our worship. Our worship can only affect our culture if we are authentic in our focus on God and the kingdom of God.

A final thought in this particular discussion of the voice and culture: Given the beauty of human diversity (diversity created by God) we should remind ourselves that the goal of Christianity and worship is not to *homogenize* the population of the globe, or our American congregations, for that matter. Rather, we acknowledge, with respect, and without apology, Jesus' great commission to *harmonize* humanity's diversity into the redeemed voice of the great congregation.

Notes

1. Walter Brueggemann, *Finally Comes the Poet: Daring Speech for Proclamation* (Minneapolis: Fortress Press, 1989), p. 4.

2. Gerard Rosse, quoted in Robert J. Karris, *Prayer and the New Testament* (New York: The Crossroad Publishing Company, 2000), pp. 103-4.

Questions for Discussion

1. Who in your congregation is generally regarded as possessing spiritual wisdom? Is there more than one person? If so, is there a consistency in their separate personalities and comments?

2. Read Numbers 13. How are minority reports received in your congregation?

3. Are there some songs and worship styles that "fit" your congregation and some that don't? Discuss this in specific terms.

4. List some songs that are new treasures for your congregation. Have they replaced old treasures? If so, what are the ramifications?

5. What is your congregation's "story"? How often and in what ways is your congregation reminded of the story? Is the story honored when changes are proposed?

6. Describe and discuss what you believe to be the "voice" of your congregation.

7. Is your congregation trying to be like another congregation in your area? Why? At what cost?

8. What giftedness, used and unused, is there in your congregation that could help bring about fresh *and* authentic worship?

9. What are some ways your congregation could be led to understand the connection between a commitment to spiritual growth and enriched worship?

10. How might your worship be more connected with the lives your members live? This question is not just about music. It is also about prayer, scripture, art, and so on.

11. Plan to worship in two or three congregations of traditions and/or ethnicities other than yours. This will enable you to look at your worship traditions with new eyes. Seeing "traditional creativity" in other settings will help you see it and appreciate it in your congregation. New ideas may well emerge in the voice of your congregation.

CHAPTER THREE

THE VOICE OF CHURCH AND CONGREGATION

O magnify the LORD with me, and let us exalt his name together.... O taste and see that the LORD is good. (Ps. 34:3, 8)

Among the most enduring works of American art is a series of paintings by Norman Rockwell entitled *The Four Freedoms*. These scenes from American life first appeared in a 1943 issue of *The Saturday Evening Post* followed by a national tour in support of the war effort. One of the paintings, *Freedom from Want*, is that of a family gathered on Thanksgiving Day as the turkey is placed on the table. Every face is smiling in anticipation, we suppose, of the feast about to be eaten.

My face during childhood was never as bright as the ones I see here. On our table were sweet potatoes, beets, Brussels sprouts, and other creations which I was certain had been cooked up by the adults to rob the joy from a child's holiday meal. D.B.

But a careful look at the Rockwell painting shows the subject is not food at all. The faces, with the exception of two figures setting the turkey on the table, are not looking at the dishes but at one another. The joy of the feast is in community—generations united by stories, dreams, and laughter—the fruit of freedom.

In this light, Mom's command to eat a little bit of everything was not an act of torture but a call to participation in family life. Most of what I know about my aunts, uncles, cousins, and grandparents I learned while passing the beets and Brussels sprouts. What was on the table (my mom really is a good cook) was insignificant compared to who was there.

I think back to the days when Julie and I were stuffing food in the unreceptive mouths of our children. We would sit on the lanai enjoying the cool tropical breeze while watching the misty clouds that hung over purple mountaintops. During those Hawaiian sunsets, we found our family. Now with both kids in college, mealtimes are different. We end up at fastfood joints, eating what appeals to our taste buds—no beets or Brussels sprouts. On the rare occasion when we actually do sit around the dinner table, I can't even remember who sits where when setting the table.

Tables are for community. Some of our Lord's greatest lessons were in the context of a meal. The feeding of the five thousand is one occasion. The miracle had nothing to do with the taste of the fish, but everything to do with people and their needs being met. The parable of the wedding banquet is another example. Why did the invited guests refuse to come? Maybe they didn't like the food. We don't know, for the point of the story is not about the menu but about who was willing to come. And of course, the greatest lesson was taught at the Passover meal when Jesus gave the new commandment that we "love one another" (John 13:34).

We had different words for the prayer preceding the Thanksgiving meal. One was "blessing," another "return thanks." The one I like best is "grace." It acknowledges the benevolent gifts of our Heavenly Father, but it also recognizes the gift by which each of us joins in the feast—eating the beets and the Brussels sprouts.

This table talk brings us to the subject of the worship service, an exercise in Christian community foreshadowing the day when the church united sits down with Jesus to partake of the marriage supper of the Lamb. Other than the new wine, we don't know what will be served, but it doesn't matter, for the joy will be found in seeing the faces of all those invited to sit at the table. Until then, in most worship services, other than those in which the Lord's Supper is shared, community centers around music; and every congregation in Christ's church can be just as picky in their musical tastes as in their dining.

As a church musician, I've long since learned how my mother felt those Thanksgiving days, slaving away in the kitchen to prepare a meal that would bring the family together. I understand her disappointment at my grimace when the sweet potatoes were set on the table, and I understand her joy with a clean plate. I had participated in the life of the family.

Each congregation is a family, and through family relationships the love Christ desires of his church is made known. After all the services, Sunday school lessons, and potluck dinners, we realize in the end that what matters most is one another. This is what Paul was teaching Timothy when he said, "the aim of such instruction is love" (1 Tim. 1:5). Likewise, the goal of church music is bringing the family together. How is this accomplished? The Thanksgiving meal analogy helps with the answer. Behind every face gathered around the table there are years of instruction in the art of eating. In the early years, each bite is spoon-fed, and the occasional tantrum may send food flying from the high chair. Throughout childhood, new foods (not always appreciated) are introduced and table manners learned. With young adulthood, nutrition becomes a concern—calories, cholesterol, and carbohydrates—learning to make healthy choices. In the end, one is not expected to become a food critic, a nutritionist, or a gourmet cook. The goal is for each family member to be nourished while participating in family life. It is also true that for every voice heard singing from the pews, there are years of instruction as well. A mother and daughter worship together—the mom, who was raised singing in church choirs, sings strongly and the daughter, for whom music is "just not one of her interests," remains silent and bored. Exhortations from the platform or changing musical style will have little effect. Singing is one activity in which this mother and daughter will not unite. As the voice of Christ's church results from the combined voices of many congregations, so a congregation's voice results from the combined voices of every generation. And yes, each generation must learn its part in the chorus. These parts are determined by the life cycle and can be described in general terms. As with all generalizations, there are exceptions—not everything will apply to every individual. In a broad sense, however, knowing the parts will prove helpful in understanding the congregation's voice.

CHILDREN

Learning the Language of Song

> Keep these words that I am commanding you today in your heart. Recite them to your children and talk about them when you are at home and when you are away, when you lie down and when you rise. (Deut. 6:6-7)

To find the most worshipful expression of a congregation's voice, we turn not to the voice of soloist, praise team, or adult choir but to the voice of a child. Be it squeals of delight or cries from a tantrum, this voice is closely wired to the heart, revealing authentic emotion. The psalmist said, "From the lips of children and infants you have ordained praise because of your enemies, to silence the foe and the avenger" (Ps. 8:2 NIV). Jesus echoed these words when cleansing the Temple, as recorded in Matthew 21. Over the course of childhood, ego, self-consciousness, and pretense will diminish this perfection; but in the earliest years, the voice most clearly recalls its Maker.

Parents and siblings have the greatest influence upon the child. From them the child will learn to walk, talk, and relate to other human beings. Musical understanding will first be gained from family members as well. The child who is sung to during infancy will learn to sing just as surely as hearing speech will result in language skills. Young children should hear music and hear it often, for this hearing will determine in large part their musical ability throughout life. Parents who don't sing may wrongly assume their child's attempts at singing indicate a special ability. Some will rush off to a music teacher for help in developing their child's unique talent. Singing, however, is a natural activity for all children and would be for adults as well if a strong exposure to music had been a part of their childhood.

Another characteristic of childhood is a rich fantasy life. Dr. Doolittle, Harry Potter, and the Brothers Grimm stretch the child's imagination to envision worlds the eye cannot see. The lines between past, present, and future are blurred and storybook characters or an imaginary friend can seem as real as the neighbor next door. Unlinked to any single time period, children happily explore music of all eras and styles appropriate to their level of understanding. They are introduced to the music of great artists—Yo Yo Ma, Paul Simon, Placido Domingo, Mahalia Jackson, Pete Seeger, Judy Collins, and Tony Bennett—through television programs like *Sesame Street,* and may attend symphony programs on school field trips. Through music, the child discovers the richness and diversity of the world. Not everyone is alike and the music they make is not all the same. American folk music, spirituals, songs from cultures around the world, jazz, blues, pop, rap, and country—all feed the child's musical imagination. He, too, will discover ways to make his own music. Listen to a child on the piano bench bang the keys then gently touch them, discovering loud and soft. Hear her furiously hit the low keys and slowly play the highs as she explores pitch and tempo.

Adults should allow children this time of discovery. Let them bang the pots and pans, sing themselves to sleep and plunk on the guitar. Give them piano lessons when older and let them join the school band. Provide every opportunity to reinforce the concept that music comes from the soul—not from electronic gizmos. Just as participating in sports develops a child's physical being, musical opportunities develop the child's imagination, inner hearing, and voice.

Parents should also be careful to expose their children to more than contemporary pop music. Kids are so cute singing and dancing to the top hits, but this should not be their only music-making experience for several reasons. First, much of this music works against proper vocal development. The child's voice at its best is light, free of a harsh, forced quality. It is resilient and unlikely to be physically harmed by loud singing (children scream on the playground). Mental concepts, however, that lead to good singing will be damaged. Voice teachers of adults must often begin by correcting vocal misconceptions formed during child-hood. Second, much of this music will no longer be sung when the child reaches young adulthood. Learning pop music with the trite tune and catchy phrase to the neglect of music rich in poetic, musical, and theological content will leave the new gen-eration ill-equipped to write their own songs of young adulthood. This is especially important in the church, for during these years children are learning the language of praise. The words they sing now will become the basis of their prayer life later on.

The children of your congregation will learn much about music through the worship services. It is here that the voice of a child meets the song of the church. True, the child will be rest-less, inattentive, and may even disturb the worshipers sitting nearby. For these reasons and more, some congregations have opted for separate "children's church" services to accommodate children's special needs. The distracted youngster, however, can absorb more from the regular worship than the most visibly devout saint. Albert Schweitzer wrote about his childhood impressions of the worship service.

> But what I loved best was the afternoon service, and of these I hardly ever missed a single one.... From the services in which I joined as a child I have taken with me into life a feeling for what is solemn, and a need for quiet and self-recollection, without which I cannot realize the meaning of my life. I can-not, therefore, support the opinion of those who would not let children take part in grown-up people's services till they to some extent understand them. The important thing is not that they shall understand, but that they shall feel something of what is serious and solemn. The fact that the child sees his eld-ers full of devotion, and has to feel something of their devotion himself, that is what gives the service its meaning for him.[1]

If the song texts are "above the heads" of the children, they will grow into them. Songs are a great way to build prayer vocabulary regardless of a few mishaps, such as the child who sang "Gladly, the cross-eyed bear" instead of "Gladly, the cross I'd bear." Though initially the lyric may not be understood in its entirety, what is understood united with a good tune will provide the sense of mystery, the "serious and solemn," that makes a deep impression on the child. Yes, a child may learn from songs other than those written for children, but the congregation should also sing songs that a child can easily understand. Sing the songs that teach about God and God's plan of salvation. Sing the songs that will bear testimony to God's providence and care throughout life. Sing the songs that help the child acquire the language of praise.

TEENAGERS

Joining the Congregation's Song

> Shun youthful passions and pursue righteousness, faith, love, and peace, along with those who call on the Lord from a pure heart. (2 Tim. 2:22)

Teens are moving—spending less time under the roof at home and more time out with their friends. Though through childhood they participated in many nonfamily activities, their basic identity was still found in the home. As adolescents, however, a new "family" increasingly shapes them. Many of their new alliances are at or near their age. Others, however, will be adults—role models they will emulate. Preferably most will be actual flesh-and-blood mentors encountered at school, on the sports field, or at church. But there will also be those known through nothing more than projected images or magazine articles—media mentors that will have tremendous influence in setting the norms by which the teenager must live to "fit in." Social standing is extremely important. No longer are there imaginary friends to confide in or control—only one's peers whose evaluations can be brutal. Even the most secure teenager will imagine her position as she wants it to be—often a fantasy—and this image becomes the guide for her behavior.

To "fit in," one must speak the language. Knowledge of the popular tunes and artists is key to joining a community that has its own voice. The language is taught by the entertainment industry willing to exploit teens' disposable income. Eager to belong and with little financial self-control, they are prime targets. The "in" music becomes the vocal instructor for teens finding their voice. On the hit television show, *American Idol,* would-be "idols" line up to sing for three professional entertainers who determine which voices are good enough to match the idol ideal. To be accepted on the show means more than having one's music appreciated: it is acceptance as a person, a validation that makes the fantasy real. Not to move on in the audition process is certainly not an encouragement to refine one's craft—it is a death sentence, a banishment from the community. The sad thing is that all of these voices have qualities that could be developed into a pleasing sound, and some could even become great. But how many young people will never sing again because the pop culture potentates pronounced they were no good? A "Christian" version of the show called *Gifted* has also been planned. Its promoter says "It is our goal to wrap God's message— God's love—in acceptance, and in a way that blends seamlessly into 'pop' culture while still upholding the values we, as Christians, value most." Eight "gifted" individuals will appear before a television audience who will choose the winner whose career (or fantasy) will be "managed" by the promoters. Hundreds of others will be rejected—an upholding of Christian values?

God's message for teenagers is that everyone is "gifted" in some capacity and everybody can belong. A congregation helps people discover their gifts, believing that God calls people to use them for God's church, God's kingdom, in special ways. This calling includes the world of artistic expression; indeed, the arts are at the heart of the calling—dance, singing, drama, the visual arts—all these and more, when nurtured and brought to life, give glory to the congregation's song. "Idols" have no place in church—the "American" or even the "Gifted" kind. Because there are many different kinds of people, there will accordingly be many kinds of expression and musical styles. Adolescents are done a great disservice when only one type of music is presented as being the only song the church sings. Even worse, they are sometimes told that in order to reach their friends for Christ they must do a certain kind of music. Teens have an ability to appreciate and perform many kinds of music, pop culture not withstanding. A large variety of offerings provides greater opportunity to discover ability.

When a Jewish male reaches his thirteenth year, he is invited to recite a blessing before the Torah is read. The blessing may be extended to include the actual reading, chant, or prayer. An African American teenager tells of her family's long-standing Thanksgiving tradition. When a girl turns sixteen, she becomes responsible for preparing the Thanksgiving meal. Planning the menu, setting the table, seating the family, serving the food, cleaning the plates—all rituals to be learned and executed. This is not forced servitude; it is a rite of passage by which the young lady becomes the custodian of the family tradition. So too, the adolescent is ready to join the voice of the congregation, and the congregation must meet that readiness with their own traditions. Opportunities may include solos, choirs, instrumental music, and dance. Teens may be encouraged to write poetry and music or even plan and lead a worship service. Though they also know the language and sing the song of contemporary culture, when guided by parents, teachers, and role models they will find joining the congregation's voice to be ultimately satisfying.

YOUNG ADULTS

Learning a New Song

> He put a new song in my mouth, a song of praise to our God.
> Many will see and fear, and put their trust in the LORD. (Ps. 40:3)

Of all the generations, congregations most eagerly seek young adults for membership. As every advertiser knows, capturing this group's loyalty is essential for the long-term success of a product or service. It is no different for congregations, particularly those with aging memberships needing new families to feed their children and youth programs, leadership demands, and financial coffers. Bring a middle-aged couple in, and you have two people soon to be on fixed incomes and in declining health. A young adult couple, on the other hand, can represent years of vitality and ever increasing financial resources. Young adults, too, are bonding with other couples experiencing the same life situations of starting a career, raising a family, and settling down. Church membership is more appealing now than in the free-floating college days, and several young families can attract many others like them.

Congregations have always had their ways of gathering young adults into the life and leadership of the family. Nuptial counseling, child-raising classes, couple retreats, and leadership mentoring programs are but a few. The practice of including members of this age group in key leadership bodies such as deacons, vestry members, and church council members also shows this intent. Two factors over the last couple of decades have complicated this assimilation process and created some panic that has its effect on a congregation's voice. For one, young adults are waiting longer to marry and begin raising a family. This is due in large part to a technical, highly competitive job market that often requires postgraduate degrees to enter the workforce. As a result, young adults often live with their parents during this extended schooling and delay establishing a career until their late twenties or even thirties. Second, this delay extends the noncommittal, explore-all-the-options mind-set of the college years, which can discourage forming ties to a particular congregation.

Because of their sought-after status, young adults can have greater influence than their numbers within the congregation. Indeed, some congregations have adapted their entire worship style to woo this age group. Other congregations have created separate services to meet this group's "needs." At times, this empowerment creates a false sense of understanding concerning the entire congregation and its voice; the belief that the church's song has evolved and can only be understood by those who are now young.

So, what are the songs that reach young adults? The easy, though questionable, assumption is that young adults only listen to the music of pop culture. Music videos, concert attendance, advertising images all associate the young with electronic, high-energy rock and rap. It is true that contemporary music by definition is the music of "now" and therefore most closely aligned with the uncertainties and challenges experienced by the young. There is a bonding, an immediate rapport between young adults brought by lyrics and melodies written for their age. Every generation has had such songs. To sing them is to go to that time and place where life appeared as a broad vista with infinite possibilities. They are songs to sing while traveling the vista, songs for the journey. Some people sing them while methodically rising above their peers to the executive suites and six-figure salaries and bonuses. Others, free spirits, sing while pursuing a good time or adventure.

But young adults also listen to other kinds of music as it speaks to their life situation, including that from the distant past. They, after all, are not the first ones to pass this way, though the landscape may have changed. There is a yearning for the deep things of life that a catchy lyric cannot speak or a trite musical phrase provide. A fascination with mysticism—both Christian and pagan—is evidence of this yearning. With more education than previous generations, young adults have more knowledge of and interest in the arts beyond the commercial. In a recent survey, 54 percent indicate a preference for traditional worship music, 45 percent a preference for contemporary, and 1 percent indicating no interest in music at all.[2]

One cannot equate traditional preference on the part of young adults as an equivalent to that of older generations. Tradition is an ocean deep and wide and not all swimmers swim in the same spots or at the same depth. A middle-aged adult may prefer Southern Gospel music as it reminds him of the church revivals of his growing-up years, while a young adult may prefer Gregorian chant for its power to evoke a place and time far different than that of the present. Conflict can occur over which tradition should receive emphasis. Difference, too, can be noted in the way in which the songs are sung. Young adults may accompany their singing with acoustic guitars, electronic keyboards, and a variety of wind instruments from flute to sax. The organ, primary to the music-making of older churchgoing adults, may be shunned as alien to an "authentic" sound in worship. Brides in increasing numbers are walking the aisle to the music of string quartets, piano, or even compact discs—while the organ, no matter how grand an instrument, remains silent. Perhaps the hymns of their childhood performed to an unimaginative organ drone have caused the instrument to fall from favor. Maybe a dozen or so gospel songs repeated ad infinitum through their youth sent these young worshipers off in search of something fresher, something more in sync with the world as they know it.

The quest for "authenticity" in worship is important to young adults. The Jesus Movement of the late sixties and seventies took worship from the sanctuary with its stained glass and candles to the beach and park—a kind of Christian Woodstock with the music sounding very much the same. The eighties moved the music from the love-in to the airwaves and music charts. Contemporary Christian artists became the music ministers with their pulpit the concert stage. In the nineties, congregations decided what was good for the concert stage was good for church. Sanctuaries that looked more like school auditoriums than houses of worship were built and equipped with large mixing consoles, computerized lighting, and video projection—all designed to deliver "authentic" worship. Gone were the hymnals, bulletins, and other printed matter with PowerPoint becoming the new iconography. And what does the new millennium bring? "Emerging worship," a return to vintage expressions with candles, stained glass, and traditional hymns.

The prophet Joel prophesied "I will pour out my spirit on all flesh; your sons and your daughters shall prophesy, your old men shall dream dreams, and your young men shall see visions" (Joel 2:28). The young still "see visions." What they see is not always clearly defined, but prophesy they must. The prophecy will be refined by life experience. Much of what is said in youth will fall away as dross—the passing fad—until only the gold of what God is speaking to his church remains. The young adult prophet Jeremiah received a word from the Lord.

> Now the word of the LORD came to me saying, "Before I formed you in the womb I knew you, and before you were born I consecrated you; I have appointed you a prophet to the nations." Then I said, "Alas, Lord GOD! Behold, I do not know how to speak, because I am a youth." But the LORD said to me, "Do not say, 'I am a youth,' because everywhere I send you, you shall go, and all that I command you, you shall speak." (Jer. 1:4-7 NASB)

Young adults are learning to speak, learning a new song to sing to Christ's church. Their speech will be unrefined, not as articulate or tactful as it will one day be. The depth and theology of their songs may be challenged by older adults and by life's experience, but at the congregation's table of thanksgiving their visions should not be ignored.

MEDIAN ADULTS

Singing a New Song

> One generation shall laud your works to another, and shall declare your mighty acts. On the glorious splendor of your majesty, and on your wondrous works, I will meditate. The might of your awesome deeds shall be proclaimed, and I will declare your greatness. They shall celebrate the fame of your abundant goodness, and shall sing aloud of your righteousness. (Ps. 145:4-7)

In the multigenerational congregation, median adults (late thirties through fifties) are often the primary leadership group. Old enough to know the church's story, they are young and energetic enough to write a new chapter. Much of what they write is in the form of meaningful program opportunities for their children. More comes from the vision of their young adult years. This vision, now forged by life experience, becomes in large part the practice of the church. Median adults' influence comes from their authority within the congregation's households. They represent their children and, in many situations, their parents as well. They are the breadwinners providing the major contributions received by the congregation. Median adults are fully aware of this majority status and may be quick to speak on behalf of the congregation.

Conflict can occur between young adults championing a new paradigm and the median adults guarding their own. Older adults have heard it all and thus may close their ears to what the young are saying. Young adults may assume median adults are out of touch with the "real world" and dismiss their viewpoint as irrelevant before fully hearing it. Often the battle is over music. Style preference of median adults is largely the same as young adults with 46 percent of median adults preferring contemporary to 53 percent favoring traditional.[3] Median adults also accept the influence of pop music on the church, believing that it takes all kinds of languages to reach all kinds of people. Differences, however, exist in the definition of "contemporary." Median adults consider all music written from their youth to the present as fitting that category, much of which may have been popular before present young adults were born. In other words, the median adult embraces songs that may have been around for over thirty years as "new," and will not easily surrender them because of the connection to their youth. It is at this point that median adults understand why their parents did not appreciate the music from the transistor radios and 45s. The resultant disharmony continues until some congregations divide into two services—"you sing your songs and I'll sing mine." Much is lost in the separation. Median adults need the fresh perspective of a world that has changed much since they were young, and the young need the refining influence that older adults can bring.

In the sixties, the middle-aged pastor of Calvary Chapel in Costa Mesa, California, Chuck Smith, befriended hippies on the beaches nearby. Many of these young adults had no place to live, so Chuck invited them to live in his home, which quickly became overcrowded. He rented another property and called it

"Miracle House." In the end, Calvary Chapel members sponsored over one hundred community homes in which many of these young adults became Christians. These new converts brought great energy to Calvary Chapel, and it was there that much of the music associated with the Jesus Movement was written.

Jim Cymbala was a young businessman in Manhattan with no long-term goals other than "just paying bills and enjoying the weekends."[4] His father-in-law, a Florida pastor who oversaw several independent churches, coaxed Jim into becoming the pastor of a small African American congregation in Newark, New Jersey. When another church in Brooklyn needed a pastor, Jim was encouraged to take it also. Today, the members of Brooklyn Tabernacle number in the thousands and its congregation's voice is heard worldwide through recordings and performances of songs written by Jim's wife, Carol.

With the postmodern era of the new millennium, multisensory experiences have become an important aspect of young adult worship. Emerging worship makes use of all the arts—drama, painting, video art, music of many styles, and poetry—in a non-linear approach, communicating biblical truth in a multitude of ways. If this type of worship is truly "emerging," the seeds for it were sown in the coffeehouse experiences of the previous generation. Books like those in the Serendipity series by Lyman Coleman[5] and *Catch the New Wind* by Marilee Zdenek and Marge Champion[6] introduced young adults decades ago to worship that was more right-brain than left-brain. Many of today's median adults have sung this "new song" in the years since, preparing the way for emerging worship.

Eli and Samuel, Samuel and David, Naomi and Ruth, Paul and Timothy, the pattern is clear—one generation mentors the next. Young adults are learning a new song and while it is unique to their time and culture, it came from the eternal song sung at creation's dawn. Median adults give definition to the younger generation's tune simply by singing their own "new song." And so the discovery is made that both songs are the same—a duet with each voice taking its turn as melody or harmony and finding that the resulting music is more beautiful than what could be known by each voice soloing in separate rooms.

SENIOR ADULTS

Teaching the Song

> Remember the days of old, consider the years long past; ask your father, and he will inform you; your elders, and they will tell you. (Deut. 32:7)

"I never could make music. That's just something you're either born with or you're not," Victor, the church librarian, exclaimed while walking past the music minister's office. "So Victor," countered the voice from inside, "were you born reading or did you have to learn?"

The retort never registered, for Victor had traveled to a place seventy years past. "I'd try to play mother's old pump organ. My feet could push the pedals, but I never could get my fingers to move; too clumsy, I guess."

Victor couldn't sing a note, but his words flowed on like music.

"Now, mother—her fingers would just fly over those keys. She'd play and pedal and sing one hymn after another."

Senior adults tell stories—stories about their youth and the events shaping it, stories about places they've been, people they've known, their children and grandchildren. The stories are also about their congregation, the pastors that have come and gone, the good days, the bad. The stories sometimes come out in the form of commentary: "this is the way we do things" or "that never worked here." They are behind the complaints about the lack of old songs, the loud organ, or the arrangement of the pulpit furniture. These comments are not necessarily intended as negative; they are like the Sunday school attendance pins of another era, a way of saying, "I belong. This is my church and my family."

Their story is a summation of life. As God rested from God's creative activity pronouncing it "good," seniors are reaching the end of their book, the satisfying conclusion of a "good read." It's a story they tell to themselves and it's a story they pass on to succeeding generations—whether or not by conscious decision, the story must come out. They may become frustrated that the setting of their story has changed. Like actors walking onto the stage and finding the set missing, seniors are thwarted in the telling of their story; little wonder the desire to slow the pace of change. And who is bringing about change, but younger generations writing their own story? Seniors want young families to join their congregation, but may resent their new stories changing the context of their own.

This holding on is reflected in worship song preferences. Seniors grew up in an era in which a distinction was made between church and popular music. They never expected that church music should sound contemporary. Whereas members of younger adult generations basically split evenly in their preference for traditional or contemporary music, 75 percent of seniors favor traditional worship music while 25 percent prefer contemporary. However, they have their own brand of contemporary that sounds like traditional church music to other generations. A hymn like "How Great Thou Art," considered by many seniors as a church music standard, was copyrighted in 1953, a contemporary Christian song of their youth. Thus, a contemporary song for a senior could be fifty years old!

The church's song carries with it more than words and melody, it carries truth and memories. The truth is about the eternal things that never change though both the song and the memories associated with it will. Word, melody, truth, and memories fuse together—impossible to dissect. No wonder then, that seniors want younger generations to sing the songs they love. The songs are a gift, which says, "here are our lives, our hopes, our dreams, our beliefs. Here is the truth that matters when it's all been said and done." In each congregation, seniors represent previous generations—an unseen majority passing on the eternal song to their children and children's children. God spoke to Moses.

> "Now therefore write this song, and teach it to the Israelites; put it in their mouths, in order that this song may be a witness for me against the Israelites. For when I have brought them into the land flowing with milk and honey, which I promised on oath to their ancestors, and they have eaten their fill and grown fat, they will turn to other gods and serve them, despising me and breaking my covenant. And when many terrible troubles come upon them, this song will confront them as a witness, because it will not be lost from the mouths of their descendants. For I know what they are inclined to do even now, before I have brought them into the land that I promised them on oath." (Deut. 31:19-21)

Senior adults are teaching the song. The song is a testimony of triumph over the disasters and difficulties of life. Knowing and singing the song will guide younger generations through the difficult circumstances on their journey. And as each generation adds their song to the church's repertoire, a "great cloud of witnesses" (Heb. 12:1) continues to sing.

Church and Congregation

An old, familiar gospel song asks, "will the circle be unbroken, by and by?" We must also consider whether the circle will remain complete in the here and now. Teaching, learning, joining, hearing, and singing the new song—each generation is needed. The congregational circle reveals the eternal nature of the church's song with young adults proclaiming the future, median adults proclaiming the present, and seniors proclaiming the past. "Where two or three are gathered in my name, I am there among them" (Matt. 18:20).

The church's song is sung as each generation is allowed to do what it does best, making its contribution while supporting rather than interfering with what other generations do. The congregation which does not allow for the song stories of its seniors makes it all the more difficult for young adults to hear their own new song. The congregation which only provides opportunity for median adults to sing their new song will prevent their youth from joining its voice.

This give and take does not come without congregational tension, and in this respect finding the congregation's voice is no different from finding one's singing voice. Muscles of inhalation and exhalation work in dynamic tension creating breath support for the voice to sound. By tension, the vocal folds stretch to varying degrees to produce pitch. Muscles of the laryngeal cavity contract in just the right amount to form a resonating cavity, which amplifies the sound produced by the vocal folds. Healthy tension is necessary for the production of the singing voice, but too much tension will work against the voice. In like fashion, healthy tension is needed for a congregation to find its voice, and each generation brings its force to bear. Balance lifts the congregation's song. If one generation pushes too hard and the other generations fall, the song falls as well.

Singer/songwriter Ken Medema performed for a largely young adult group in Louisville, Kentucky. A special part of his concert came when he asked the audience members to volunteer stories about meaningful times in their lives, and then made up impromptu songs about them. Whatever an audience member gave him, he gave back in song, so polished that it sounded as though he had spent hours composing. A senior adult stood to speak, leaving no doubt as to her unhappiness with this segment of the concert: "Can't you sing something else?"

The atmosphere in the room became tense.

"Right now, Ma'am, I'm asking for stories. Do you have one you could give me?" the singer politely asked.

"We didn't come here for that. We came to hear some hymns," came the taut reply.

"What is your favorite hymn?" responded Ken.

"How Great Thou Art," she said, softening.

He gently prodded, "Why is it special to you? Is there an experience you associate with it?"

Her voice broke, "I remember my dad would set my little brother on his knee and sing this song to him when he was so ill."

Without another word, Ken masterfully played an introduction then began singing something like "Withered hands, tender hands lifts a child upon his knees." He continued to paint a beautiful song picture of two generations, a grandfather and grandson, intertwining "How Great Thou Art" with new music and lyrics that told the story. The woman cried, as did most of the audience. What had begun as an uncomfortable moment had been patiently and skillfully transformed into a memorable, moving experience.

Each generation holds something of God's song gift. From the "ordained" music of children to the song stories of senior adults; when generations unite, the congregation's voice is heard. "What should be done then, my friends? When you come together, each one has a hymn, a lesson, a revelation, a tongue, or an interpretation. Let all things be done for building up" (1 Cor. 14:26).

Every Sunday, your congregation gathers at the table. Maybe the bread is broken and the cup passed weekly in the supper Christ bids us share. If not, the gathering is still an act of community not unlike the Thanksgiving meal. A deacon said, "I don't have much to say about the music, but if my children and grandchildren are helped by it, then that's good enough for me." His words of grace expressed a willingness to enter in community even if the music didn't appeal to his musical taste buds. The early church called their gatherings "love feasts." They were fed as much by their relationships as by the actual food. The apostle Paul warned the early church about losing the love over musical food fights. "If I speak in the tongues of mortals and of angels, but do not have love, I am a noisy gong or a clanging cymbal" (1 Cor. 13:1). Good manners should always be used at the Lord's table.

Before concluding this chapter, we must take another look at Rockwell's *Freedom from Want* to notice two images that could be considered metaphors for the work of the worship leader. The first is the focal point of the painting. An elderly couple, we assume the begetters of this family, are placing the Thanksgiving turkey on the table. Doing so, they are not looking at the family members but at the platter. This bird was prepared in a hot oven according to a recipe refined through the years until the combination for just the right moisture, just the right tenderness, just the right seasoning was found. It is lowered to the table with care and a sense of ceremony in honor of the many Thanksgivings past when the same ritual was performed. The second image appears in the lower right corner just inside the frame. A partial face turns to the viewer, the smiling eyes beckoning "come, take your place at the table." Whether you're a child, teenager, young to median adult, or a senior, it's the face of your favorite uncle saying you belong. So, too, the worship leader has two faces. One face stares intently at what is being served, and the other looks away from the table. One face looks back to what has been and is now, while the other looks out in anticipation of what will be. Some of the people standing at the table's edge will sit down adding their voices to those already at the table. Others, however, would rather stand and remain hungry—hymnals shut, mouths unopened, eavesdropping on the conversation but unwilling to join the celebration. No matter the response, pastor, choral director, organist, or song leader with one face surveys the table's ample feast and with the other face beckons saying "Dinner's ready!"

Notes

1. Albert Schweitzer, Kurt Bergel, and Alice R. Bergel, *Memoirs of Childhood and Youth* (New York: The Macmillan Co., 1955), pp. 44-45.

2. Jackson W. Carroll and Wade Clark Roof, *Bridging Divided Worlds: Generational Cultures in Congregations* (San Francisco: Jossey-Bass, 2002), p. 231.

3. Ibid.

4. Jim Cymbala and Dean Merrill, *Fresh Wind, Fresh Fire: What Happens When God's Spirit Invades the Heart of His People* (Grand Rapids: Zondervan, 1997), p. 12.

5. Lyman Coleman, *Encyclopedia of Serendipity* (Serendipity House, 1976).

6. Marilee Zdenek and Marge Champion, *Catch the New Wind* (Waco, Texas: Word Books, 1972).

Questions for Discussion

1. Examine the texts sung by the children of your congregation. Which ones will they continue to sing throughout life?

2. What opportunities could your congregation provide to highlight the talents of your youth? There's nothing wrong with talent shows other than the kind that limits diversity.

3. Are there service responsibilities that could be performed by youth of a certain age as a rite of passage?

4. Take a group of young adults on field trips to services of other congregations. Be sure to include both members of your congregation and nonmembers. Gather after each service for a debriefing. What did the group find meaningful? What was not meaningful?

5. What songs do the young and median adults in your congregation have in common? What songs particular to each group could be meaningful to the other?

6. Rather than just singing seniors' favorite hymns, find out the cherished memories associated with them. Ask a senior to tell a story to the congregation before each song is sung.

CHILDREN	ADOLESCENTS	YOUNG ADULTS	MEDIAN ADULTS	SENIOR ADULTS
Identity shaped by parents and siblings	Identity shaped by peer influence and role models.	Identity shaped by recent events and mentors.	Identity shaped primarily by the events of youth.	Identity shaped primarily by the events of youth.
Highly imaginative. Enjoy fantasy and blur distinction between past, present, and future.	Imagine their place in the world as they want it to be.	Imagine the world as they want it to be. Fantasize the future.	Remember the world as it was and imagine it the way they want it to be.	Remember the world as it was and imagine it as it will be for the generations to follow.
Enjoy all music appropriate to their level of understanding and ability. Learn about music through improvisation.	With continued exposure, enjoy and perform music of many styles; otherwise favor the music of pop culture.	Most familiar with contemporary music. Appreciate music from the past as it enriches the present.	Most familiar with contemporary music from past decades.	Most familiar with contemporary music from past decades (50-year gap with young adults).
N/A	N/A	Unlikely to differentiate between pop and church music.	Accept the influence of pop music on the church.	Differentiation between pop and church music.

Think a legacy of Christian song should be passed from generation to generation.	Think all kinds of languages are needed to reach all kinds of people.	...should reach the world in today's language.	music of many styles.	
Represent themselves and previous generations.	Represent the church membership.	Represent the unchurched masses.	Represent young adult families and the church's future.	Represent enthusiasm and energy in the church.
May resent change while desiring younger generations in their congregation.	Realize the "new" comes and goes. Guard the paradigm of own youth.	Establish a new worship paradigm.	Observing the congregation's worship.	Joining the congregation's worship.
74% favor traditional worship music; 24% favor contemporary (not always the same the same choices as young adults); 2% prefer no music.	47% favor contemporary worship music; 53 % favor traditional (not always the same choices as young adults).	54% favor contemporary worship music; 45% favor traditional; 1% prefer no music.	N/A	N/A
Consider the piano and organ as primary. Opinion mixed on the use of other instruments.	Enjoy a diversity of instrumental sounds including the organ.	Enjoy a diversity of instrumental sounds. May consider the organ alien to contemporary culture.	Enjoy a diversity of instrumental sounds.	Enjoy a diversity of instrumental sounds.

CHAPTER FOUR

THE VOICE OF PULPIT AND PEW

I will tell of your name to my brothers and sisters; in the midst of the congregation I will praise you. (Ps. 22:22)

Walking down the narrow alleyway leading to Tumen Church in Xi'an is like walking back into old China. On this early Sunday morning, a young worker pulls a wooden cart loaded with bricks as produce peddlers set up their stands of fruit, fish, and vegetables. How odd our group of Texan singers in tuxedos must look, walking down this dusty alley with its crumbled walls and broken windows. A small boy runs across my path. He is headed for an outdoor sink where he fills a small container with water. His smile accessorizes a light patterned sport coat and dress shirt—his Sunday best. I stop and take his picture. Just then, I notice the happy sounds of other children's voices descending from the second story of a drab brick building—singing, laughing, and learning. Sitting on a bench against the large ivy-covered church sanctuary is a group of elderly Chinese men and women. They smile; I wave and snap another picture.

At 7:15 A.M. our group walks into a building that is already filled to capacity (all five hundred seats) while many other people crowd against the walls or in back doorways. They are simple folk, dressed in dark clothes—blues, blacks, grays, and browns—who have been sitting in wooden folding chairs and on benches since 5:00 this morning. Their early arrival was not to hear the Americans sing, for they assemble like this every week in expectation of God's presence. We awkwardly shuffle into our rows of chairs beneath the pulpit. High above the chancel area are Chinese characters and a cross. The words, someone says, are "Emmanuel, God with us." They describe what I am seeing, hearing, and feeling—a congregation of Chinese believers sitting on hard seats for two hours before a service even starts because they believe that God is here. From somewhere to my left come distant voices of choir members—rehearsing because they also believe God is here.

After ten minutes of sitting silently with this unusual congregation, the choir director walks briskly into the room. Taking a seat on the piano bench, his fingers strike the keys—like a child improvising, he pounds with a certain artistic flair, which signals the choir. They process down the aisle dressed in white robes with pink and red stoles. Following close behind are a young woman and an elderly Chinese man with a kind face. Both wear black robes, as they are the church pastors. The service has begun.

Listening to the congregation in its forceful, staccato affirmation of praise, followed by the singing of "Holy, Holy, Holy" in Chinese, makes me wonder about our services back home. Why doesn't everyone sing as they do here? We add our English version of the hymn, "All thy works shall praise Thy name in earth and sky and sea," rising to the wooden arches, out the windows, up to heaven.

The fervency of this Chinese congregation is born out of oppression. The last century brought civil war, the Japanese invasion, Communism, and the Chinese Cultural Revolution, during which the church buildings were turned into factories and the ministers assigned secular jobs. Persecution, however, failed to silence the Chinese church's voice. Today, 48,000 gathering places exist for some 15 million Protestant believers under the leadership of the China Christian Council. A common story, hymnal, and liturgy has brought forth a common voice among the many congregations, and to Western ears, the enthusiastic hymn singing and recitation of scripture at a church in Shanghai sounds very much like a service in Beijing. The Chinese sing songs of triumph: "Joyful, Joyful We Adore Thee," Mozart's "Gloria," and "All Hail the Power of Jesus' Name."

American congregations, too, at times have shared a common story. Wars, economic depression, and national celebrations have challenged and rejuvenated Christians' faith, giving congregations of different persuasions something to sing about. September 11 was one such occasion. Congregations across the land gathered in special services to recite Psalm 46 and sing hymns, such as "O God, Our Help in Ages Past." Even senators and congressmen of both political parties united on the Capitol steps in a rousing rendition of "God Bless America," an event unlikely to be heard or seen again. Most of a congregation's stories, however, originate closer to home. There was the time the mill closed down and folks lost their jobs; there was the afternoon the tornado hit the town square. There were the revival meetings, weddings, dinners on the grounds, the pastors who came and went. A thousand events, like these and more, shape the identity of a people banding together to face the uncertainties of life with the belief that God is in their midst.

In a bygone era, people were born, grew up, worked, and died in the same town. They attended one of several churches where they sang from the same hymnal each service. Every couple of decades, the denominational publishing house would produce a new hymnal drawn largely from the songs of the previous one with some new hymns added. These new songs would work their way into the congregation's song vocabulary as they fit the congregation's story. Few people were shy about singing. Children learned the hymns by imitating the adults and thumbing through the hymnal during the long sermons. (One child memorized all the hymn numbers and titles this way, and today teaches church music in a major university.) The songs voiced the congregation's theology and told their story—not so much with words but by association of tune and text with time, place, and people. From the simple songs of testimony to magnificent hymns of praise, eternal truth was committed to heart and mind and sprang forth when prompted by the circumstances of life.

Other than in a few rural communities, only senior adults remember those days (and the old-timers in your congregation likely do). Today's congregation is a mix of people from many places with many stories and many songs. Each member has a sacred repertoire comprised of songs from other congregations, from camps, Bible conferences, and Christian radio. Add to this variety the dynamics of multiple generations meeting together, and it's understandable why musical tensions can exist within a congregation. How do you go about selecting songs the congregation sings, the songs that tell its story?

On television's Learning Channel is a hit show called *What Not To Wear.* Persons with no fashion sense are selected to be on the show and receive a complete new wardrobe and makeover by fashion experts Stacy and Clinton. Laura, a young mother, was nominated for the show by family and friends who observed she always hid her beauty under sweatpants and waffle shirts. After receiving a consultation from Stacy and Clinton, Laura was sent to the mall with $5,000 to spend. Through a hidden camera, the experts watched with amazement as she selected the same big, baggy clothes they cautioned her to avoid. Laura was repeating the same fashion mistake, afraid to wear clothes that really fit. After a good scolding by Stacy and Clinton, she made better choices and in the end was completely thrilled with her new look.

If a congregation makes poor choices in the songs it sings, its voice will be diminished. Here are questions the congregation should consider when selecting its songs.

1. Is this a song our congregation can sing well? Are there complex rhythms, meter changes, intervals that make the song better suited for a soloist?

2. Do the music and text of the song work together to reinforce the themes presented through the sermons and teaching ministry of the congregation? Is the song true to the theology, practices, and story of our congregation?

3. What is the context in which the song will be used? Is it right for the space where it will be sung? (What sounds good in a large auditorium with pipe organ accompaniment may not be effective in a country church. Select songs that are right for the room.)

4. Will the poetry connect with the congregation's imagination? (The hymn "Come, Ye Thankful People, Come," with its harvest and winter imagery may hold little meaning for a Miami congregation.)

5. Will the song continue to be sung by succeeding generations? (Fads change. Listen to some old LPs of popular church music from twenty years ago. Does the music still have its impact? Add to your congregation's repertoire music that will continue to teach and inspire the members throughout their lives.)

6. Do our songs express the wide range of experience and emotion of the Christian life? (The Psalms contain expressions of both praise and lament. Are there songs your congregation can turn to in times of triumph and trial?)

7. Do our songs represent the diversity of God's creation? (It's impossible to reflect the music of every culture and style, but there should be enough variety in the music that people of different musical backgrounds can feel at home.)

Selecting the songs for any given service and the order in which they're sung is largely the responsibility of whoever stands in the pulpit in consultation with the poets and prophets who sit in the pews. Some of the selections the congregation will know well and sing strongly. Other songs may be less familiar or unknown. Look at your congregation in its worship and you will see a variety of responses as the songs are sung.

- A few of the members appear disinterested, mouths closed, maybe eyes shut. (Certainly this isn't what the voice looks like!)
- Others are trying to sing but seem to be having a rough go of it. (Is a worship service any place for teaching music, or wouldn't everybody be better able to worship by singing something everyone knows?)
- And then, some people are singing with abandon—not even looking at the hymnal, song sheet, or overhead screen, but to where angels and saints gather before the throne of God. (Now this is more like it—the true worshipers worshiping in Spirit and in truth.)

While hearing all voices given to song is an exhilarating experience, songs exist for reasons beyond the actual singing. Worship songs exist to renew the mind of the congregation and to transform (Rom. 12:1-2). They must reach deep, renewing the mind and transforming everyone who stands in the pulpit or sits in the pews. A few well-worn songs won't do that anymore than a few well-known phrases can suffice if one is to live in a foreign country and understand anything significant about its culture. To speak German, for example, requires that one first listen to German being spoken; next will come awkward attempts at forming the vowels and consonants that make the sounds. If you really want to learn to speak German, however, you will travel to Germany and live with Germans until fluency is gained. At this point in the process, you will be able to converse without laboring over every word—your mind will have been "renewed." You will speak like a German; you will be "transformed." The process, however, will not end here. Inflections, innuendos, the traditions and the depth of the vocabulary will continue to renew and transform until one day, perhaps, you will think in German instead of only speaking it. Song is a musical language to be learned and you can observe people in various stages of learning in your services.

Stage One: Hearing the Song

"Listen! I am standing at the door, knocking; if you hear my voice and open the door, I will come in to you and eat with you, and you with me." (Rev. 3:20)

God spoke a word to the seven churches of Asia through God's servant John, who was exiled on the isle of Patmos. It was a word of grace and revelation of Christ's coming. But this word was not the last word spoken by Alpha and Omega. To each of the churches God spoke a special word of exhortation and blessing according to their individual stories. What was true then is true now. The word of grace and revelation still comes—a word all can share in and a word that springs from each congregation's story.

How does a congregation know the word God is speaking to it? John Gutzon Borglum, the man who carved Mount Rushmore into the likenesses of Washington, Lincoln, Jefferson, and Theodore Roosevelt, once explained how he went about the mammoth task of sculpting. "When I carve a statue, it is very simple. I merely cut away the pieces that don't belong there and the statue itself presently comes into view. It was there all the time." A similar statement can be made about God's word. It is incarnate, present in the life of the congregation—calling out in the pulpit and the pews. The word cries out through the church calendar with its special observances and seasonal events. It sounds from the doorways of children's Sunday school departments and round the tables in fellowship halls. Listen and you will hear it in the memories of past accomplishments, and the stories of brothers and sisters who once sat in the pews and moved away or went on to heaven. The word will be heard in missionary reports, prayer requests, camp testimonies, and business meetings. Not everything you hear will be the word; but through all the noise the word will sound forth as surely as the statue presents itself out of the rock. In Hebrews 2, Jesus calls us his brothers and sisters and says, "in the midst of the congregation I will praise you." Think of it—when your congregation sings this Sunday, Christ is there with you singing in the pews.

God's word for God's church as well as God's word for your congregation will occupy the pastor in sermon preparation. If he or she has prepared well, a word from the pulpit will summon forth the living word known by those who sit in the pews. Deep does call unto deep. In the same manner, God's word for God's church and congregation will occupy the church musician in music selection and preparation. In the case of vocal music, the poet hears the word and responds to it out of her life experience. The composer hears the poem and joins it with music. As God's word to the church at Ephesus is a fitting word to other congregations as well, so the church musician will hear in songs written in other times and places a word meant for their congregation. These are the songs he will teach the choir, soloists, and other musicians. The goal is not finding the right combination that will suit the congregation's style preferences, but finding the word that is lived out in the pews—the deep calling to the deep.

The congregation will welcome and with their voices give back the songs that resonate with the word they are living. The church musician must look everywhere to find them. The Psalms, Latin hymns, Greek hymns, the hymns of the Reformation and of Watts and the Wesleys; high church and low church, spirituals and *Sacred Harp*, praise and worship, contemporary Christian— all these sources and more can yield songs that will be sung and treasured by the congregation. The church musician understands that no one generation can write all the music that will convey the Word in all its height, depth, and breadth. Like the woman searching her house for the lost coin, the church musician must search until the songs suited for the congregation's voice are found (Luke 15). Go ahead and begin in the corner you think most likely, but search the whole musical house!

Before rushing out to begin the search, consider why music is so important to the hearing of God's word. In his introduction to a choral collection by Georg Rhau, Martin Luther observed: "the gift of language combined with the gift of song was only given to man to let him know that he should praise God with both word and music."

Why will it not suffice for the word simply to be spoken? Consider this. Neurologists observe that the right and left hemispheres of the brain process different types of information. Generally speaking, the left brain processes cognitive information and the right brain the emotional/affective. Music imagery is dealt with in the right hemisphere and its analytical components in the left. Receiving a song, the left side analyzes the text and the right processes the emotional content. Thus, the hymn "When I Survey the Wondrous Cross" will convey to the left hemisphere the language "see from his head, his hands, his feet" while the right hemisphere deals with the emotions associated with Christ's death. Music helps us to know the truth beyond what words, in the cognitive realm, can tell us. We may learn by the words how Christ died, but the music carries a deeper knowledge to levels of consciousness where mere words cannot go. For this reason, church musicians often argue that music is more than preparation for the sermon; it, too, is proclamation, and some worshipers will attest that they get more out of the singing than the preaching. Music does prepare the mind, however, to receive the spoken word. Dr. Arthur Harvey, music education professor at the University of Hawaii and executive director of Music for Health Services, observes how music is used as a therapy in health care to make the mind more receptive.

> To deal with stress, the use of specific types of music were found to alter states of consciousness. Using biofeedback techniques and disciplined mediators, research showed activation of alpha brain activity patterns. Alpha brain waves produce a conscious state of relaxed wakefulness which dominates over the problem-solving state.... If music can be identified that will cause subjects to respond with increased alpha brain wave activity, then that music would be a valuable therapeutic vehicle to help them attain the relaxed receptive state.[1]

The book of 2 Kings tells of a time when the kings of Israel, Judah, and Edom sent for Elisha. There was no water and their armies were facing a catastrophe in their battle with the king of Moab. The three kings asked Elisha for a word from the Lord. Elisha replied, "Bring me a harpist." As the harpist played, God told Elisha how water would be provided. The music prepared Elisha to receive God's word.

There are harpists in your congregation—musicians whose skill can prepare your people to hear God's word and sing in response to what they've heard. The development of that skill and the knowledge of how to use it is crucial to the hearing and the singing. Some people have wrongly suggested that a seminary education is not as important for the music minister as for the pastor and could hinder the Holy Spirit by making the musician more interested in music than in ministry. A "sparkle," an engaging personality, a quick wit, and nice hair has been known to outrank a magna cum laude degree as qualification for leading God's people in song. But, who should teach the language of praise other than one who knows the intervals, rhythms, tonal colors, and dynamics of the musical art? Who should listen deeply to the congregation's voice and know the inflections, the call of its tradition and ministry to the community it serves? A little "sparkle" can't hurt, but if the ones who sit in the pews are to resonate deeply and fully with God's voice, then the one who stands to lead must be a student of theology, worship, and music. "How are they to call on one in whom they have not believed? And how are they to believe in one of whom they have never heard? And how are they to hear without someone to proclaim him?" (Rom. 10:14).

The service planner hears the word and imagines how the elements of the service will proclaim it. The choir, instrumentalists, and soloists rehearse the music to "cut away the pieces that don't belong" until God's word "presently comes into view." When the musicians make their music, the congregation will hear God's word and their own voice in what is sung and played. Hearing the word and the voice prompts the entire congregation to join the song and to join Christ who praises God in its midst. For this reason, hearing is as important as singing. Be thankful for the people who are not singing in your congregation as well as the ones who are.

Stage Two: Rehearsing the Song

"It is good to give thanks to the LORD, to sing praises to your name, O Most High." (Ps. 92:1)

Barbara rarely attended church as a child. Her mom was Catholic and her dad a Methodist. One summer in her teen years, a friend invited her to church camp where she asked Jesus to come into her heart. There was never any follow-up on this decision, and all she ever knew about the church was what she learned at camp. The years passed; Barbara married and had two kids. She wanted for them the church experience she never had, so she and her husband agreed to visit a Baptist church near their home. Walking up the church steps on Sunday morning required a degree of courage. Barbara felt like an intruder crashing another family gathering. A friendly couple at the door with big smiles and warm handshakes helped put her at ease, but on the other side was a foyer filled with strangers who knew the right way to dress and all the right things to talk about. Barbara's family hurried through the crowd into the sanctuary finding a spot in a pew midway back on the right. The service began. Barbara thought, "Okay, we'll be all right as long as we do what we're told or what everyone else does." When the music minister announced the first hymn, she dutifully reached for a hymnal. The organ accompaniment was majestic, the choir's voice strong, and with her best voice she attempted to sing a song she had never heard out of a hymnal she had never opened. As the music grew in intensity, she even began enjoying herself and decided to go for the high note at the end of the refrain. That was the last thing she would remember about the service. When she hit the note, it was like she had walked onto a dark stage and a spotlight had suddenly turned on her before an audience of strangers. To her horror, she realized no one around her was singing. She knew that her husband wouldn't be—he had never been a churchgoer, but the family sitting behind them who seemed to know everybody and the greeters they met at the door had not even opened their hymnals. Maybe she had misunderstood.

The psalmist sang, "You are my hiding place; you will protect me from trouble and surround me with songs of deliverance" (Ps. 32:7 NIV). Where do the songs come from that surround and offer protection to the stranger in the pews if not from the congregation? Silence its voice, and the hiding place disappears. The Swiss-German theologian and pastor Karl Barth observed:

> The praise of God which constitutes the community and its assemblies seeks to bind and commit and therefore to be expressed, to well up and be sung in concert. The Christian community sings. It is not a choral society. Its singing is not a concert. But from inner, material necessity it sings.... What we can and must say quite confidently is that the community which does not sing is not the community.[2]

The building of a church sanctuary (as well as the building of community) begins with commitment but does not end there. Following the commitment comes the construction process. The same is true about music. "Making" music is exactly that—a process. The congregation must not stop with hearing the song, but move on to rehearsing the song, recognizing that God has bequeathed a voice, not only an ear. It's easy to get stuck in stage one, merely hearing; every congregation has people who've been stuck there for years. Why is this so?

One reason is that music making is largely considered to be a special ability, a talent, possessed by those born with it. This wrong notion has even been preached from the pulpit (the parable of the talents is a favorite text): "You may not be able to sing, but God has something else you can do!" The problem with this teaching is that scripture contradicts it. Why not say, "You may not be able to pray or read the Bible, but God has something else you can do!" Singing is one of the basic disciplines of the

Christian life. True, some people can do it better than others, but the voice of the congregation is the voice of "many waters," the voice of many voices, and not the voice of "good" voices alone.

Among other reasons voices stay silent is the tendency of worshipers to disconnect from the service. They've heard it all before, so they use the time to daydream. Unresolved conflict in a congregation can also squelch the spirit of worship. Paul said that the gatherings of a congregation divided cause more harm than good (1 Cor. 11:17). Nevertheless, before the dreamers and the dividers, the one in the pulpit stands. He or she joins Jesus at the door of people's hearts and calls forth the song.

There is an art to song leading. In the sixties and for several decades thereafter, a trio of folk musicians taught America to sing. Peter, Paul, and Mary sang the songs of the country's heartland and of its heart. They sang both songs of brotherhood and protest, songs so powerful that people on both sides of the war issue claimed the songs as their own. At a Peter, Paul, and Mary concert, the audience lost all resistance to singing. Housewives, business professionals, grandparents, long-haired hippies, and school children joined voices—even singing about a magic dragon named Puff. What is this magic? Composer and hymnologist Alice Parker suggests that in every good song there is something unique, something that can touch the soul. The job of the song leader is to "hunt" for it; for when that something is found, the soul of the congregation will be touched and its voice given.

The hunt begins at the same place it did for the composer— with the text. Read the words silently to understand what they are saying. Read the words aloud to understand them as poetry. What is the meter, the phrasing, the inflection, the tone colors, and nuances that convey the truth beyond the words? When you have found the answers, you will have an idea of how the composer came to hear the tune; you will understand the tune's subtleties beyond its notation. It's possible you may even hear a different tune that reveals something unique that only you have heard. The text is the place where choir, solo, and praise team should all begin their rehearsal as well. Rehearsing the text, they will understand the music before they even sing a note. Once they do sing, they will reveal to the congregation the uniqueness they have discovered—that which touches the soul. The same rehearsal process can help the congregation. Nonsingers especially will find text recitation a less threatening way of worship participation. Encourage the congregation to find the music in the text—reading it with the right inflection and phrasing rather than the drone that groups can easily fall into. If it's not appropriate in the service time to point these things out, use an accomplished reader to lead the group. It's a short step from poetic reading to song.

A tune is not inspired by text alone. It is a product of time, place, people, and all the other tunes known by the composer. In this sense, tunes are the work of community. The composer will be influenced by songs sung to her as a child, taught to her in school, and sung around the campfire. She will also be influenced by music heard in her travels and through her formal education. If she lived two hundred years ago, the tunes she wrote would be sung differently from ones written today. If she grew up in Appalachia, her tunes would be accompanied differently from those of a composer in the Austrian court. Is this too obvious a statement? One would think so, but congregations for the most part neglect this fact, singing their songs as though they were all written in the same time period and location.

> All too often we take the hymnal for granted. Because each page looks alike, we tend to think that the music should sound similar, that is, in a neatly inclusive "church" style, which will offend no one, and not attract too much attention. A quick glance at the dates and geographic origins of the hymns demonstrates that there can be no such thing as one common hymn style. These tunes and texts are as diverse as the societies which produced them, and with a little imaginative effort, we can begin to recreate their original function and sound, and thereby make the music alive again.[3]

Making the music "alive again" in a sense makes the people who first sang it alive again also. We join them in their song and find their song becoming our own. That's why unaccompanied folk song can be so engaging. That "something" that touches the soul lies near the surface and stirs primordial feelings within us. As a song is altered through the years by generations that never knew how it was originally sung, the "something" becomes buried in layers of tradition. At times the alterations improve the song; more often, they obscure it, making the "something" harder to find. The song leader must therefore go back to the song's origin. Was it sung fast or slow, loud or soft, with piano, guitar, bongos, or no instruments at all? Tone quality, tempo, instrumentation are all factors to be considered before rehearsing the song with choir and congregation.

Once these questions are answered, there is the fun part— inviting people into the song. The manner of invitation is another decision to be made by the one who stands in the pulpit. Some song leaders have a short rehearsal time prior to the service. I once attended the service of a Chinese congregation who had arrived an hour early to learn a new hymn. Each phrase was sung by the leader and echoed back by the congregation until the entire hymn was learned. This method, known as "lining out," can also be used within the service in less apparent ways.

1. A soloist sings or an instrumentalist plays one stanza before the congregation sings.

2. Women sing a stanza while the men listen and then switch.

3. Phrases are sung antiphonally. For example, on the hymn "Come, Christians, Join to Sing," the congregation sings the "Alleluia, Amen" phrase in answer to the other phrases sung by the choir.

4. The congregation sings an ostinato—a short, simple recurring pattern—while a soloist sings the tune.

Another method of inviting the congregation into a song is to ask everyone to hum the tune. This will be the least threatening approach for nonsingers and will allow everyone to experience the melody before marrying it to the words. Whatever method you choose, expect the singing to be light as the song is rehearsed. Prompting the congregation to "sing it like you mean it" is inappropriate at this stage. The Bible tells us little about Jesus' early years other than that he "grew in wisdom and stature, and in favor with God and men." The day came when he spoke like no man had ever spoken, but his speech was acquired over the span of thirty years. So too, the people who sit in the pews need time to rehearse their voice. Begin by reading, move to humming, and finally to singing. Through this process you are helping people to do what they instinctively want to do—to sing, though they may be unaware of it. We have all been created for song.

Some years ago I was invited to direct the music for a Dallas congregation while its music minister was on vacation. Being a stranger in the pulpit, I was uneasy about starting the first song. The congregation stood, the instruments began to play; I gave the preparatory beat for the congregation's entrance, and then came a loud groaning coming from the pews. My first thought was that someone was having a seizure. I quickly surveyed the sanctuary hoping to see an usher attending to the situation, but no one moved. For a panicked moment, I considered stopping. Then I realized—standing on the left side of the room was a group of young people with special needs. What I had heard was not groaning; it was singing! These extraordinary singers were exuberantly praising God, adding a thrilling dimension to the congregation's voice. God told not only the musically gifted to sing God's praises. God told us all. We are to "hear" the word and then learn to sing it!

Stage Three: Living the Song

"How blessed are the people who know the joyful sound! O LORD, they walk in the light of Thy countenance." (Ps. 89:15 NASB)

The gain from hearing God's word and learning to sing it is far greater than good service music; it's in knowing the "joyful sound" wherever we go. We carry the sound with us as we are filled with the Spirit and make melody in our hearts to the Lord (Eph. 5:18-19). God listens to our hearts even as he looks upon them. To sing the song and to live it is why we were made. The "joyful sound" brings light, health, and God's blessing.

An interesting story is told about the work of Dr. Alfred Tomatis, an ear, nose, and throat specialist. During the sixties, he was asked to examine a group of ninety monks at the Bec-Hellouin Abbey in France. The monks, who normally were very industrious, had become lethargic and slumped in their cells like wet dishrags unable to work or pray. There was no apparent medical cause for their malady, but Dr. Tomatis did discover that a short time before it began, a new abbot had ended the traditional six to eight hours of Gregorian chant the monks engaged in every day. All that singing, in his opinion, wasted too much time. Dr. Tomatis started the monks singing again and in nine months' time, all but two had returned to their daily schedule of work and prayer.[4]

Songs refresh, renew, and charge the psyche, giving us energy for work and prayer. They also teach us how to work and pray as we encounter life's challenges and difficulties. The psalmist sang, "I have hidden your word in my heart that I might not sin against you" (Ps. 119:11 NIV). When we hear and rehearse a song, we are planting God's word deep within our consciousness. Like a perennial plant, it will spring to life again and again to help us in life's changing contexts. Jamie is a young mother who sings in my choir. She wrote this note to her music minister about Tom Fettke's anthem "The Majesty and Glory of Your Name."

> I just wanted to let you know how meaningful the music was yesterday in worship.... I first heard "The Majesty and Glory" when I was about ten years old. I first sang it in youth choir when I was maybe fourteen. I sang it in my college choir a couple of times, and I've sung it in almost every church choir I have been in as an adult (six churches including the present).

Yesterday I was moved to tears while singing because I heard this piece in a different place and time in my life. I keep hearing the line "little children praise you perfectly, and so would we" repeating in my thoughts. As a mom I sometimes have the opportunity to "listen in" on my children. They break into worship in some of the most unusual places and they are often oblivious to their surroundings. They offer their praise to God in the most pure form of worship. They give themselves fully and it does not matter to them who is listening. Oh, to be like little children and sing praise to God while not being concerned about what anyone else thinks. Thank you for providing an opportunity for a familiar song to breathe new life into a sometimes cynical and often weary soul.

There is another aspect to the song we carry in our hearts, and that falls in the realm of mystery. We've discussed how music communicates a text's emotional content, but it can also be a vehicle by which God comes to us. This incarnate dimension to music was realized in the Temple worship detailed in 2 Chronicles.

> The trumpeters and singers joined in unison, as with one voice, to give praise and thanks to the LORD. Accompanied by trumpets, cymbals and other instruments, they raised their voices in praise to the LORD and sang: "He is good; his love endures forever." Then the temple of the LORD was filled with a cloud, and the priests could not perform their service because of the cloud, for the glory of the LORD filled the temple of God. (2 Chron. 5:13-14 NIV)

God comes to us in song! You have likely had that experience. It's not unusual. It happens often when a heart is tuned to God, though some experiences may be especially memorable. One Sunday night when I was a child, about seven years old, the children in our congregation learned a little chorus based on John 3:16.

> For God so loved the world He gave His only Son
> To die on Calvary's tree, from sin to set me free.

Someday He's coming back, what glory that will be!
Wonderful His love to me.[5]

Walking to the church parking lot, I was humming this little song and looking up at the night sky. Beyond the song came the perception of another voice speaking not in words but in truth. "Yes, I am returning." I shuddered—not out of fear of being harmed, but because I sensed an awesome reality beyond myself. Jesus was singing through the song.

Jesus said, "My sheep hear my voice. I know them, and they follow me" (John 10:27). The Voice speaks through Bible study and prayer and grows stronger as we love our neighbor. The Voice also speaks to the songwriter as he sets poetry to music and to the singers as the resulting song is heard, rehearsed, and lived. Songs are not the Voice or representations of the Voice, and to consider them so would be idolatry. Songs are, however, a place of communion where the Voice can be heard. This is why church musicians are sometimes fussy about their music; they are listening for the Voice in the song. And it could also be said that one who does not listen is one who has never heard.

Stage Four—Singing the Song

> Praise the LORD! Praise God in his sanctuary; praise him in his mighty firmament. Praise him for his mighty deeds; praise him according to his surpassing greatness! Praise him with trumpet sound, praise him with the lute and harp! Praise him with tambourine and dance; praise him with the strings and pipe! Praise him with clanging cymbals, praise him with loud clashing cymbals! Let everything that breathes praise the LORD! Praise the LORD! (Ps. 150 NRSV)

Every singing congregation wants a Psalm 150 voice—a loud, exuberant voice singing with abandon joyful songs of praise. A congregation's theology, tradition, size, or style does not matter. A strong voice is the voice of conviction, evidence that the congregation believes what it has been taught to be true. There is an energy that comes with such singing, inspiring the congregation in its work of worship and ministry. As preface to the 1543 *Genevan Psalter,* John Calvin wrote: "In truth we know by experience that song has great force and vigor to move and inflame the hearts of men to invoke and praise God with a more vehement and ardent zeal."

The motivational power of music is not only a Christian understanding. The ancient Greek philosophers spoke of *ethos,* a doctrine that separated music into two types—one producing calmness and the other excitement. Music was selected according to the god being worshiped—meditative music for Apollo and high energy for Dionysus. Why does music have this power? Dr. Arthur Harvey explains.

> One of the more "popular" explanations is that the neuropeptide, endorphin, an endogenous opiate that affects moods and blocks pain receptors, is stimulated by music (as well as by other means) and that, in turn, music is responsible for changing emotional states. Music may also trigger recall of "positive" emotions that are stored in the subconscious.[6]

Music affects us physiologically whether it comes from a gospel singing convention or a hard rock concert. God made us this way. Though God-given, music's emotional charge is not evidence of God's coming in a special way. Christians, however, can become addicted to musical energy, equating it with God's presence. The authors attended a "live worship" event led by Darlene Zschech and Hillsong, a high-energy worship team from Australia. Down the row from us a woman in her forties fidgeted in her seat, anxiously waiting for the program to begin. She held a cabasa, a Latin rhythm instrument, keeping the beat against her palms to prerecorded music coming from the loudspeakers. She was primed. When Hillsong did begin their music, she shot out of her seat and began a high-spirited dance as she waved a tambourine. The music was beyond deafening—meant to be felt rather than heard—and the tambourine dancer, along with many others in the crowd, was lost in the sound of praise. Interestingly though, after about twenty minutes the woman sat down in her chair physically spent. She listened and prayed.

Like the ancient Greeks, congregations may fall into one of two musical camps—the meditative or high energy. The first thinks of music as a conveyor of truth to be heard and considered, the other thinks of music as the force moving and inflaming the heart to praise. Paul asks, "What should I do then? I will pray with the spirit, but I will pray with the mind also; I will sing praise with the spirit, but I will sing praise with the mind also" (1 Cor. 14:15).

Mind and spirit are both required. Without the mind, the songs cannot convey the truth, and when the music dies, we are left empty and emotionally spent. Without the spirit, we may never be moved to hear, rehearse, and live the songs, and there again, the truth will not be known. So, Paul tells us that to sing with both mind and spirit, three types of music are needed: "Let the word of Christ richly dwell within you, with all wisdom teaching and admonishing one another with psalms and hymns and spiritual songs, singing with thankfulness in your hearts to God" (Col. 3:16 NASB).

The Psalms teach us the language of worship and guide us in meditations that are pleasing to God. Hymns teach us from the life experiences of other believers and congregations who have walked with God and lived the song. Spiritual songs teach us to sing with abandon, pouring out our emotions of joy and lament as offerings at God's feet.

The congregation is to sing all three types. Each works to bring the voice to maturity, a Psalm 150 voice singing songs that have been heard, rehearsed, and then lived. The prophet Amos delivers a blunt word from God about our singing. "Take away from me the noise of your songs; I will not listen to the melody of your harps. But let justice roll down like waters, and righteousness like an ever-flowing stream" (Amos 5:23-24).

God demands more than an exuberant song. God calls for a righteous song that springs from the hearing of God's word, rehearsed by every member of the congregation, then lived and sung. Everything else is just noise. In his preface to his 1761 hymnal, *Select Hymns*, John Wesley laid out rules for singing.

> Above all sing spiritually. Have an eye to God in every word you sing. Aim at pleasing him more than yourself or any other creature. In order to do this attend strictly to the sense of what you sing, and see that your heart is not carried away with the sound, but offered to God continually; so shall your singing be such as the Lord will approve here, and reward you when he cometh in the clouds of heaven.[7]

Engaging the Song

The search committee was wrapping up its meeting with a promising candidate for the church music position. Everyone was smiling. His was an impressive résumé; he had satisfactorily answered their questions, and it appeared that their search was coming to an end. The chairman had just begun to review the next steps in the hiring process when the senior member of the group, who until this point had remained curiously silent, spoke up. "Not so fast," he interrupted. "There are a few things I want answers to." The committee members cringed. Sam always had to have the final word, and here he was having it again. He had purposely waited to ask his questions until the most conspicuous moment. Embarrassed, they all slumped back into their chairs as Sam unfolded two sheets of notebook paper and fired off the first question. "How do you get people to sing?"

It was just the kind of question Sam could be expected to ask. Church to him was getting people to do what they really didn't want to. Giving their money, attending Sunday school, bringing their friends—all these were on the list to which "getting people to sing" had just been added. The answer, of course, is that people are going to do what they want to do. Even if they don't want to give their money, attend church, or sing, they will do so because they "want" to live up to someone's expectations. This type of "want to" is not the same as "knowing the joyful sound" or "making melody" in one's heart to the Lord. To this type of singing God replies, "Away with the noise of your songs! I will not listen."

Becoming the kind of singer that God will listen to and delight in is a process. It begins with hearing, leads to rehearsing, then living, and finally singing. The congregation cannot be made to sing, but they can be invited to enter the stage of growth for which they are ready. Among the members of your congregation, you can observe all four stages. Whether singing enthusiastically, barely moving the lips, or reading the song lyrics, all can engage the song at the stage that is right for them. The one who stands in the pulpit helps those who sit in the pews to engage the song.

Engaging the congregation in song is much like hosting a party. This is an analogy that Jesus once used when referring to God's kingdom. At a good party everyone meets old friends and acquaintances along with people they have not met before. In similar manner, the worshiper will be put at ease if she encounters music she already knows and enjoys. She will sense that the service is a place she belongs and will consequently be more receptive to new introductions. The host remembers, too, that the guests come from different backgrounds with varying degrees of education and life experience. He will see to it that each guest can share from their background without either being looked down on or intimidating others. Some worshipers are just beginning to voice their praise while others are "putting away childish things" and speaking "meat." No one, however, should be made to feel childish. More mature Christians will show their maturity by accepting and singing the songs younger believers find meaningful. Comments like "these choruses lack depth" can squelch the life of the party.

When the guests engage in conversation, everyone should get their turn. There is a time for inquiring, a time for listening, and a time to speak. Only a boor will do all the talking. The leader guides those who sit in the pews to sometimes listen, rehearse at times, and at other times sing. Unless a song is newly composed, all the worshipers will not engage the song in the same way; some in the congregation will sing while other members listen. Give every group an opportunity to sing something they know and thereby teach the rest of the congregation. This is in keeping with Colossians 3:16 to "teach one another with psalms and hymns and spiritual songs."

The host keeps a party fresh with mixers or games that help the guests discover something new about one another, even about their closest friends. Old, familiar songs should be kept fresh as well. Try changing the tune by uniting the words of one hymn with the tune of another in the same meter. Vary the accompaniments through the use of congregational hymn arrangements and free harmonizations. Drop the instruments and allow the congregation to hear its voice without accompaniment. All these techniques and others can bring a congregation back from the singing stage to rehearsing and hearing, where they may again hear God's voice in the song.

Good planning is required to host a party, and it takes thorough planning to engage a congregation in song. A good planner does not call attention to herself for she knows that congregational singing is a community activity. When she has planned well, those who sit in the pews engage more than the songs, they engage one another.

Before ending this chapter, let's return briefly to another analogy used earlier—that of carving rock. The Galleria dell'Accademia in Florence, Italy, is a "must see" on any European tourist's itinerary. Under its dome stands the eighteen-foot-high statue of Michelangelo's *David*, a Renaissance masterpiece. The work is truly remarkable in that the marble block Michelangelo was given to use had been damaged years earlier. Michelangelo worked according to the principles of *disegno*, believing David's image was present in the flawed stone in the same way the soul was encased in the human body. The mammoth statue stands in marked contrast to the sculptor's other work found in the museum. Four unfinished statues intended for the tomb of Pope Julius II, *The Captives*, illustrate how Michelangelo worked—chipping away at the marble until the subject he imagined was revealed. Uncompleted, these twisted forms fight against the stone that enslave them. Meant to stand free like *David*, they are forever slaves to the rock.

Like Michelangelo looking for the subject in the stone, the church musician listens for the song in the congregation and chips away at all that holds the song captive. Some Sundays, to human ears, the song may seem fettered; the congregation's voice silent. Other Sundays, the song will seem to rise unencumbered, joining saints and angels in their song of praise. Whichever the case, the church musician guided by the Spirit chips away through layers of hearing, rehearsing, living, and singing, knowing that God hears what mortals cannot. God is the One for whom the congregation's voice resonates and for whom its song is sung.

> To thy majesty, O God, ten thousand times ten thousand
> bow down and adore, singing and praising without ceasing
>   and saying,
> Holy, holy, holy, Lord God of hosts;
> Heaven and earth are full of thy praises;
> Hosanna in the highest.[8]

Notes

1. Arthur Harvey, "Music Soothes the Troubled Soul..." *Ad Nurse* (March/April, 1988):19.

2. Karl Barth, *Church Dogmatics IV*, Part 3, trans. G. W. Bromiley (Edinburgh: T&T Clark, 1961), 866-67.

3. Alice Parker, *Creative Hymn Singing* (Chapel Hill: Hinshaw Music, Inc., 1976), 6.

4. Tim Wilson, "A l'ECOUTE de l'UNIVERS: An Interview with Dr. Alfred Tomatis," *Musicworks* 35 (Summer 1986).

5. Frances Townsend, "For God So Loved the World," © 1938, renewal 1966 by Alfred B. Smith, assigned to Singspiration, Inc.

6. Arthur Harvey, "Music and Health," *International Brain Dominance Review* (Fall, 1987).

7. John Wesley, "Directions for Singing," no. VII in *The United Methodist Hymnal* (Nashville: The United Methodist Publishing House, 1989), vii.

8. From the *Nestorian Liturgy*, 5th century.

Questions for Discussion

1. What are the significant events in the life of your congregation? Are there special songs associated with those times?

2. Compile a listing of the songs sung by your congregation over the past year. Are there many songs expressing the breadth of congregational life or a dozen or so repeated throughout the year?

3. What are the themes that keep emerging in your congregational conversations that reveal what is important to the people and perhaps to God as well?

4. Review an upcoming service order. Is there a narrative connecting the service elements? Are there elements that should be discarded? What might God say to the congregation? What will they say (sing) to God?

5. Why not start singing classes for all ages in your congregation, including the adults?

6. In an evening service, dim the lights to near darkness. Following a time of silence, ask the members to choose and begin singing a song in which the rest of the congregation can join. Have several singers ready to begin the process. The congregation will sing as prompted by God's Spirit—a moving experience.

7. Does your congregation fall into the meditative or high-energy camp? Do you sing primarily scripture texts, hymns, or spiritual songs? Which type should you sing more often?

CHAPTER FIVE

THE VOICE OF HERE AND HEAVEN

And I heard a loud voice from the throne saying, "See, the home of God is among mortals. He will dwell with them; they will be his peoples, and God himself will be with them; he will wipe every tear from their eyes. Death will be no more; mourning and crying and pain will be no more, for the first things have passed away." (Rev. 21:3-4)

This chapter is about hope and hopelessness. The voice of the congregation is the voice of hope. Even a "dying" congregation that has lost hope in themselves clings to the hope of heaven. That hope is often housed in their liturgy and its music. Therefore, to take away their hymns (or choruses or worship songs) is to attempt to wrench their best hope, perhaps even their last hope, from their hands. To make major changes in their liturgy or their "order of service" or their worship style (the three terms are interchangeable from tradition to tradition) is to dismantle the structure upon which they stand. For many, changing the music of worship is the same as changing the structure of worship. Notice how many times the word *their* is used. The congregation knows that they have a corporate or community voice, even if they have never spoken of it in those terms.

It is a strange thing to see clergy and laity, who have the best interests of the life and work of their congregation at heart, become angry with congregation members who are "dragging their feet," or "resisting change." Perhaps they are merely defending their hope, and will do so, until they are convinced that that hope is not at risk. Rather than seeing these members as enemies of progress, they should be seen as the first ministry to be performed in the process of progress. Dismissing the "old" congregation to make room for the "new" congregation, as if we were talking about laundry loads to be moved from washer to dryer, is not how church is supposed to work. Have we not learned from the worship wars that fighting and division are not worth the resulting distraction from, and destruction of, worship? Dismantling the place, procedures, and/or music of hope of one group to establish it for another is prejudiced, judgmental, and, in the end, self-serving. Change must go at your congregation's pace, in tune with the voice of your congregation. If it doesn't, you are simply setting up the new converts to "the Way" of Christ to be treated in similar fashion when the next new worship or music style comes along and is touted to be "the way" to worship. Living in the here and now with integrity will keep us from doing damage in the present congregation in preparation for an imagined future congregation.

The Voice and Community

Worship connects your congregation with the church universal. Isolation, the feeling that your congregation is alone or has been left in the dust as others move forward, can lead to hopelessness. It ignores the connectedness that exists between your congregation and all others. A congregation that is in touch with its own voice and is confident in its own mission, and its giftedness toward that mission can see growth in other congregations and be glad rather than jealous. There is a difference between learning from other congregations and making an idol of them. A congregation's hope can be found in its uniqueness. The unique voice of your congregation can be an important contributor to the welfare of your larger community and an important contribution to the combined voices of the congregations in your area. We are to be brothers and sisters in Christ and in community, not clones of one another. This is not a license to be smug and lazy. It is a call for your congregation to be itself as gifted by the Holy Spirit.

There is great hope in this kind of congregational self-understanding. Being in touch with the voice of your congregation will allow you to work at doing a better job of making your contribution instead of trying to imitate another congregation's giftedness. Sometimes it is difficult to concentrate on being faithful without being distracted by the desire to be "successful." There are many examples of growth, even numerical growth, in congregations that continued to be faithful to God and to themselves without ever trying to simply imitate other congregations. An example is DaySpring Baptist Church of Waco, Texas. (Such examples are certainly not confined to Baptists. This is simply a reflection of the authors' experience.) This congregation, some ten years old, has been until recently small in number. They were determined not to worry about numbers and growth. Rather, as their motto states, they would concentrate on worship that is "Sacred, Simple." They did not change their worship style or its music; they simply gave themselves to discipleship and worship in the context of their giftedness. Their e-mail newsletter included the following encouragement from the pastor, Dr. Burt Burleson:

> Okay, so everyone's got their consciousness raised, right. We're all aware that there are new folks in the room on Sunday who for sure need our friendship, who may need our seat, and who'll probably take our parking place.
>
> "Peace be still." There is nothing to fear. God is with us. Remind yourself of that as you head to church on Sunday and have to park in the grass. I know, it's frustrating introducing yourself to the same person three times. I know, you miss not knowing everyone but there's nothing to fear. God is with us. Remind yourself of that when you offer your hymnal to a visi-

tor who can't find one. I know it's not ideal doing Lectio Divina with a baby screaming. Peace be still. God is with us. Remind yourself of that when you see young parents being nurtured during our worship time. (This would include taking a nap during the sermon.)

We're growing at a rapid rate for a church our size. And we have some "growing pains" to deal with but these are good problems to have and there really is nothing to fear. It's not like we're going to become a megachurch and build a bowling alley—maybe a golf green or a racquetball court—but no bowling lanes. We have to draw the line somewhere.

We have never been a church that focused on numbers, so don't start. Focus on people and peace. Be still.[1]

One can only hope that no other congregations will see the growth of DaySpring and decide that being a DaySpring is the new way to grow. The "secret" is being who God has gifted your congregation to be; knowing the authentic voice of the congregation and refusing to be derailed by numbers. The core or voice of the congregation can withstand the pressures of numbers, great or small. DaySpring is in concert and harmony with the other congregations in its town. For the first several years of its existence, it met in the facilities of a local Seventh Day Adventist congregation. It is not in competition with other Christian communities. The congregation knows its voice and has not changed it. Those who are joining are attracted by authenticity, not by fad or even by novelty.

An important aspect of the DaySpring community is that the voice of their congregation is one of unity in harmony, not forced unison. The congregation is made up of members from a number of faith traditions with differing political opinions. What they have in common is a need for healing and a desire for worship unencumbered by the agendas of the kingdom of this world. They sing music they know and music that is new to them without fretting or fussing. They open themselves to the text of the songs. The style of worship is one that causes everyone, no matter their worship background, to say this is new, but strangely familiar. Only the Holy Spirit can make that happen. Their growth is grounded in the work of the Holy Spirit, not in niche marketing;

in authenticity, not desperate imitation. Worship wars do not ignite in such an environment.

The Voice and the Story

When a congregation finds its voice, it finds its place in our segment of the ongoing and overarching story of Christianity; a story that arches from Genesis to Revelation, from Heaven to Earth. Do you want to carry your congregation's part of the story in some other congregation's voice? No segment of the story should be undertaken without some thought given to the story of redemption that led to your day and your congregation. Will the story that goes forward, having passed through your day and your congregation, remain authentic?

A congregation that is considering a change in worship/music style should begin by purposefully and publicly reminding itself of its story and its authentic contribution to the overarching story of God's work in the world. The congregation's story, in combination with the story of Christianity, is the only foundation upon which change can be solidly built. Further, such a rehearsal of the story will put minds at ease that might otherwise fear the congregation's history and heritage are about to be discounted or forgotten. Such a recounting of your congregation's story is easily, if not quickly, accomplished. Consider having a fellowship meal during which members, especially the older members, are encouraged to share their remembrances. Ring the walls of the fellowship hall with butcher paper upon which appear the years of the congregation's history. Allow members to go to the appropriate section and write their name under the year in which they became members. While there, encourage them to write short statements of significant events in the life of the congregation, in which they participated.

Many congregations have enjoyed this kind of remembering activity. It honors the past and those who worked to make it happen. It establishes a communal understanding of the historical environment in which new developments in worship will take place. In a sense, this kind of purposeful remembering draws a picture of, or narrates, the story of the development of the voice of the congregation. Significant stories in the congregation's past can be published in the congregation's newsletter. Be sure that some of those significant moments relate to worship. Examples might be the adoption of a new hymnal, the establishment of a new choir, or the installation of a new organ. Honoring the past brings about trust and a context for future changes. Publishing inexpensive history books and performing plays that tell the congregation's story are additional ways in which the past can be learned or remembered, honored, and built upon. These activities will not derail progress, they will greatly enhance the prospects for peaceful and effective progress that ministers to the congregation along the way. This may be slower than dictated change, but what's the hurry? What's the cost of hurry? We know the cost of worship wars. We must take the time necessary to work for, and in, peace. We must work to maintain authenticity in worship.

Change in the context of the authentic voice of the congregation will not require the congregation to "take up arms" in order to defend the congregation's past (including worship/music style) or in order to ensure an envisioned future. The honored past and the envisioned future will be at home in the present understanding of the story of God's work in the world and your congregation's contribution to, and participation in, that story.

There is hope to be found in the vast company of believers that occupies the overarching story of God's work. There is hope to be found in understanding that you are a part of a community of Christian traditions and congregations of which your congregation is but one. There is work for your congregation to do; the authentic work for which your congregation has been gifted. There is worship for your congregation to offer to God, worship that is authentic, thus offered in spirit and in truth.

The Voice and Citizenship

We are, most assuredly, citizens of the kingdom of this world *and* the kingdom of God. Taxes *and* tithes are a part of our economic lives. Prayer *and* protest are a part of our community lives. Grace *and* greed find a place in our hearts. Our dual citizenship causes us to seek ways to accomplish heavenly goals and worldly goals at the same time.

Dual citizenship is not easy, for the simple and obvious reason that divided loyalty leads to duality. Duality in our lives will have us speaking out of both sides of our mouths. No person, no congregation, can speak truthfully in two voices. We have it on good authority that we cannot serve two masters (Matt. 6:24). One of the kings in our dual citizenship ultimately has to be subservient to the other. Our worship, its focus and motivation, will be given to one or the other of the two kings. The King of the kingdom of God admits to a divine jealousy that will not tolerate the worship of other gods (Exod. 20:1-8). The rather clear phrase, "No other gods," *should* make voicing authentic worship easier for us Christ-followers. But the truth is that it doesn't. That's because we have trouble drawing the line between doing something *for* God and giving worship *to* God. To pose it as a question in our current context: When does changing our voice to bring people *to* God in worship prevent authentic worship *of* God? The voice of the congregation is an important thing to know. We cannot do authentic work or worship with an inauthentic voice. When our two citizenships clash, our voice will reveal our true loyalty.

The voice of the congregation can learn new expressions. We've acknowledged that fact several times in these pages. Like an individual, a congregation is capable of learning a new language while maintaining their original language and their natural voice. Even though a person speaks English in one conversation and Spanish in another, their voice remains the same. They can speak authentically in both languages. Their identity does not change. Can you imagine the absurdity of a person using one voice to speak English and another to speak Spanish? The assumed voice would be heard as mocking the language, perhaps even mocking the culture that produced the language. The lack of authenticity would be repulsive. Our voice must be *our* voice, no matter which language we are speaking.

This allows for changes in worship, but only changes within the boundaries of authenticity.

No matter where the authors of this book speak, we speak as Americans. Our conversations are heard through the filter of our American citizenship. Should we imply another citizenship by what we say or how we say it, our authenticity and our credibility would disappear. Think of a strained attempt at a British accent. Now think of that phony accent being used in conversation with a British person in London. If we are perceived as trying to be *of* this world in our worship, people could draw the conclusion that we believe the gospel we are living *in* this world might be too weak to speak in its own voice. This doesn't mean that a congregation should not ever make adjustments in their worship style or music. But it does mean that the change must be within the parameters of their authentic voice. Some existing worship styles might seem silly if attempted by your congregation.

Seekers are seeking something different. If what they find in our worship is what they already know, they must keep seeking. They hope there is a difference between "here and heaven" or else they wouldn't be seeking something different in our congregations. Authenticity is, or should be, one of the big differences. Authenticity is a rare commodity in this world. The voice of the congregation must sound forth in its worship, a certainty of faith that marches toward heaven, making its way through the uncertainties of this world. There is no room for voice *impressions* in the preceding sentence. If we are to be the Body of Christ, to be Christ's hands and feet continuing his ministry on earth, we must have the voice to match.

Jesus, our model, was fully human and fully divine, the perfect example of how to handle dual citizenship. Jesus worshiped within a given structure. He was a Jew and he worshiped as a Jew. He did not set out to change the structure of worship. He came to fulfill it. He did not set out to make worship more appealing. He simply made the profound statement that he was the fulfillment of the prophecies read and studied by the Jewish people for centuries. Something happens to worship when Jesus becomes alive within it. No need to import any external motivation devices or strategies. No need to look for something more relevant. However, we must be aware that the new wine will probably have an effect on the old wineskins. But that change is internal. That's the stuff of heaven expanding the stuff of here, not the other way around. The voice of the congregation must sing the songs of heaven. But the acknowledged presence of Jesus will fulfill the prophecies and testimonies of the old songs and can well be expected to produce some new sounds as well. Citizens of heaven make a difference while they are citizens of this world. If the difference isn't present they may be hiding their true citizenship. Only the authentic voice of the congregation can show the world what heavenly citizenship looks and sounds like.

The Voice and the Message

The message is this: our God is real and the gospel is, indeed, good news. That message cannot be proclaimed with integrity, or convincingly, when spoken and sung in a false voice. We have already established the fact that we cannot worship the real God in spirit and in truth using imported music and worship. We can learn and adopt, but even then not everything will fit our voice. It's true of our worship and it's true of our proclamation. We know when a new and creative idea is really just a gimmick. If we feel the need to ask if it's a gimmick or not, it probably is. The question rises from the depths of our soul and our conscience. We should trust questions and thoughts that come from there. Few people would feel good about using gimmicks to trick people into worshiping God (as if that could actually be done). Gimmicks rely on "near truth" rather than *the* truth. If we know that about worship, both its music and its proclamation, we should also know it about the integrity of our music and worship style. The gospel does not need to be propped up. It does not need to be drenched in dazzling lights. It is, actually, quite simple. We are called to simply live the gospel and be honest in our worship. I heard one worship leader confess, "I'd stand behind the pulpit and throw jellybeans out into the congregation if I thought it would liven up worship." What would the message be at that point? Thankfully, there was no indication that he actually did that. The "gimmick question" would have served him well. I don't know of any congregations who would claim that such an act would represent the voice of their congregation and what they thought about worship.

If our worship sends the message that we are selling something and that that something is so lacking in quality we need to throw jellybeans to sell it, we have nothing of value to proclaim. Worship on holy days and holidays would be reduced to "holiday sales." The voice of reason questions such activity. The voice of the congregation, taking the voice of reason one step further, rejects, intuitively, any silliness that cheapens worship. Well-meaning pastors and worship leaders should respect this built-in safeguard. Poorly thought out change in worship and/or music style could disconnect the congregation from their voice and make them seem unsure of the strength of the gospel they preach and live.

The voice of the congregation, that "knowing" in the "pit of our spiritual stomachs," is the Holy Spirit whispering that we are straying away from the gospel and its simplicity. It is an urging toward renewed trust in the Holy Spirit, trust that has us listen for the Spirit rather than speak for the Holy Spirit. The title of this chapter is "The Voice of Here and Heaven." The Holy Spirit knows both places and knows them better than we do. If the Holy Spirit is perceived to be "missing the boat" and missing opportunities for success "here," it may be because the Holy Spirit knows better than us what matters in "heaven." The voice of the congregation is in tune with the Holy Spirit—yes, even your congregation. The voice of the congregation is often lost in the din of naysayers and over zealous champions of the newest methods. That does not mean that the voice of the congregation does not exist. It certainly doesn't diminish the importance of the message that might be buried with the voice, decibels below the surface.

It is important to remember that the closer we get to the gospel message the more authentic and humble our voice becomes, even when it is expressing joyous worship. At the same time, our lives increasingly glow the gospel. "Forbid it, Lord, that I should boast, save in the death of Christ, my God; all the vain things that charm me most, I sacrifice them to His blood."[2]

The gospel message informs and shapes the voice toward the authenticity of the message. To ask the authentic voice to be silent while a more successful voice is sounded forth is to change from God's message to our message. To ask the authentic voice to be silent while a more successful voice is sounded forth is to suggest that the Holy Spirit may be working on the wrong agenda, a mistake that we will correct. The voice of the congregation and the gospel message are connected. They are connected at the point of authenticity: the authenticity of the simple gospel.

The Voice and Hope

In the opening sentences of this chapter we encountered the dynamics of hope and hopelessness. The hope of heaven is a gift, in and of itself. Slaves sang of heaven. It was the only hope they had here. That hope, and the faith that accompanies it, was often their only possession. They traveled light as they were "just a-passin' through." Singing, "this world [was] not their home" was not a way of dealing with death, it was a way of dealing with life that would have, otherwise, been hopeless. It was straight from the heart and straight from the voice of their congregations.

One of the ways to reconnect with the voice of the congregation is to listen for expressions of hope that emerge from the congregation as a whole, groups from within the congregation, and/or individuals within the congregation. The voice of the congregation is characterized by expressions of hope. The Holy Spirit often speaks through the congregation and there is nothing hopeless about the Holy Spirit. Songs or styles of worship that disconnect the congregation from their hope cannot be understood to be the voice of the congregation. They will sing, even learn, new songs as long as the new songs connect with their hope: the hope of heaven in the future, and the hope of God's strength in the present.

It is a serious matter to decide for your congregation as a whole, or for the older people in your congregation, that some of them are going to have to be "sacrificed" for the sake of progress. Some people may leave when change happens, even change that remains in the context of the voice of the congregation. But that leaving doesn't have to be a divorce. It can be a time of blessing those who are leaving, blessing them in their decision. If they won't stick around for the blessing, you can still pray for them. But such partings should not be counted a victory or smugly assigned to the inevitable cost column. When the voice of the congregation is honored in change, that voice will call to those who are not convinced. We all have seen older people in the contemporary service. That is because they still hear the voice of the congregation, even in a service that does not feel comfortable to them. The opposite is true as well. Younger people will often detect the authentic voice of the congregation, the voice of the Spirit's blessing, in the midst of the older folks and their music. They worship there because of the authenticity and for the hope that is so present and dynamic.

An atmosphere of hope is not only enriching for believers and their worship, it is magnetic to nonbelievers who know hopelessness all too well. Jesus, in whom is our hope, said, "And I, when I am lifted up from the earth, will draw all people to myself" (John 12:32). The phrase is *lifted up*, not *propped up*. The voice of the congregation is a voice of hope. Seemingly hopeless congregations have lost touch with that voice. When they find it, by lifting Jesus up, the hope will begin to glow in the darkness of the world around them. That is not a baptized cliché. The truth of it has been proved over and over again. When Jesus is lifted up, with no other agendas allowed, the promise of the scripture is fulfilled. Often, hopelessness has come about because the people have worked themselves to "death" making Jesus and the gospel be what they wanted them to be. For years they have jumped ahead of the Spirit's timing, trying to answer their own prayers, just in case Jesus couldn't or wouldn't. This is not preaching. It is a report based on experience. Doesn't it ring true at some level in your heart? The authentic voice of the congregation speaks this hope into the congregation and into the world.

People without hope will do just about anything for a glimmer of hope. Ten million to one odds in state lotteries prove that. For many, hopelessness is worse than death. The voice of the congregation will be a voice of hope, real hope, hope in and through the resurrection of Christ. That's how you can identify the voice. That voice will worship in spirit and truth because hope is one of the tenants of the kingdom of heaven. Taking a chance on gimmicks, methods, and marketing is a tenant of the kingdom of this world. "The kingdom of the world has become the kingdom of our Lord and of his Christ, and he will reign for ever and ever" (Rev. 11:15 NIV). That hope is heard from "loud voices in heaven" in the Revelation to John, the triumphant voices here on earth singing the *Messiah* of Handel, and the deep, foundational voice of the congregation—the voice of here and heaven.

The Voice and Peace

Much of the division that led to the recent worship wars can be traced to arguments over where to place our hope. Knowing that, we can avoid a return to worship warfare by returning to hope in Jesus and the truth of the gospel. We do not have to manufacture external hope when the hope of heaven is welling up from within us. The voice of the congregation reflects that understanding and seems to demand the internal hope while rejecting attempts to import external hope. If worship wars came about, in part, from congregations looking at and "shopping for" several differing worship options outside their worshiping community, peace can come by looking for worship renewal *within* their worshiping community. The voice of the congregation will not lead to warfare, but to peace, because all involved will recognize the voice of the congregation as their voice. Unity will come by the simple actions of worship and speaking the truth.

Worship unites, agendas divide: it has been written and preached before. Championing particular outside worship styles and musical styles will often lead to division. That division can lead to serious conflict. But worship held in common and expressed in the common, deeply held voice of the congregation will unite. This is not a guess. It is a report. (Or as the unfortunate old joke goes, "This isn't preaching, this is the truth.")

There is much healing to be done in many congregations. Seeking to find the voice of the congregation can be a path to peace. Discovering and celebrating the voice of your congregation can be a declaration of peace. Consider these words of James:

> Who is wise and understanding among you? Show by your
> good life that your works are done with gentleness born of wis
> dom. But if you have bitter envy and selfish ambition in your
> hearts, do not be boastful and false to the truth. Such wisdom
> does not come down from above, but is earthly, unspiritual,
> devilish. For where there is envy and selfish ambition, there
> will also be disorder and wickedness of every kind. But the wis
> dom from above is first pure, then peaceable, gentle, willing to
> yield, full of mercy and good fruits, without a trace of partial
> ity or hypocrisy. And a harvest of righteousness is sown in
> peace for those who make peace. (James 3:13-18)

Notes

1. Dr. Burt Burleson, excerpt from DaySpring Baptist Church, Waco, Texas, e-mail newsletter, September 9, 2004.

2. Isaac Watts, "When I Survey the Wondrous Cross" in *The United Methodist Hymnal* (Nashville: The United Methodist Publishing House, 1989), no. 298.

Questions for Discussion

1. Discuss changes in worship that you have witnessed that may have been done too rapidly. How might change take place in your congregation without causing damage?

2. Is it possible that instead of something new, your worship simply needs a renewal of its original meaningfulness? Discuss.

3. What are some of your congregation's strengths and unique qualities? How can these be enhanced to become more meaningful in your worship?

4. Which of the ideas suggested here would work best in your congregation? What additional ideas would you suggest?

5. What are some ways that your congregation has cooperated in ministry with other congregations of your tradition, other Christian traditions, and other faith traditions? Plan to do more of this, but this time, be especially aware of your congregation's contribution. It will help you recognize the voice of your congregation, and its importance.

6. Discuss, without being judgmental, some worship practices you have seen or heard about that would not be acceptable in your congregation. Why would they not be acceptable? Do the answers point to your voice?

7. Isaac Watts's "When I Survey the Wondrous Cross" is referenced in this chapter. Look for other hymns, choruses, and modern worship songs, as well as songs from other cultures, that also contain this message of humility before God and the gospel. Discuss whether or not the songs you find fit the voice of your congregation. If so, how might they be presented as a common body of songs for your congregation's worship? How might these songs lead to a greater sense of community in your congregation?

8. Discuss the concept of the acceptance or rejection of new songs as an identifier of the voice of your congregation. How does the way the new songs are introduced affect this "experiment"?

9. In question number 7, you sought out songs of humility before God and the gospel. Now repeat that same exercise, focusing on songs of hope. Ask the same discussion questions.

10. If you are reading this book as a group, have one person read James 3:13-18 aloud, twice, while the rest of the group closes their eyes and listens prayerfully. Then allow five minutes for silent reflection. After five minutes, share with one another what the Holy Spirit revealed to you in this passage. If you are reading this book alone, read the passage aloud, twice, then spend five minutes in silence, considering what the Spirit revealed to you in the passage.

EPILOGUE

Our stewardship of the voice of our congregation requires us to teach our children that there is such a voice. It requires us to help them know and discern the voice. Our stewardship of the voice of our congregation requires us to transfer ownership of the voice to our children as they mature in Christ and in churchmanship. What, then, shall we teach our children?

Our children belong to God. Our parenting and teaching, therefore, are acts of stewardship. As stewards of these precious gifts from God, we are to train our children in the context of our obedience to God. This does not mean that we are to mold them into the image of God. We read in Genesis that God has already done that. Our additional attempts would border on the idolatry of creating an image of God. We are, however, to train our children toward Christlikeness. Do you see the difference? We are to train our children toward *Christ*likeness. There is an important distinction between molding our children into the image of who or what we want God to be and raising them up toward Christlikeness. Do we want our children to grow up acting like they are God Almighty or humbly praying to be more Christlike? Do we want them to use worship or to be transformed by worship? Do we want them to pretend in worship or to be authentically present in worship? Of course, we want them to be authentically present in worship.

What shall we teach our children? We will answer that question here and now and then spend the next several pages explaining the answer. What shall we teach our children? The answer is this: *Let us teach our children what we used to know, but have somehow forgotten.* I apologize for any unintentional echoes of Robert Fulghum's book, *All I Really Need to Know, I Learned in Kindergarten.*

We have somehow forgotten that worship is about God and that God is worthy of the very best we have to offer.

We have forgotten that what worship *costs* us is more important than how worship *comforts* us or how it *serves* our agendas. We should not lift up to God worship or any other offering that costs us nothing. Let us remember, and then teach our children, that if worship costs us nothing but is fashioned to comfort our needs and preferences, it may not be worship at all. We know that, but it seems we have somehow forgotten it.

Let us remember, and then teach our children, that a congregation is a community and that in a community we must learn to *give* and take, not just take. This includes singing songs that are the favorites of others, even if they are not our favorites. Let us remember, and then teach our children, the importance of humility and respect toward other people. Let us remember, and then teach our children, that God can and does speak through individuals in the congregation and through the congregation as a whole, as well as through the pastor. We know that, but many congregations and pastors seem to have forgotten it along the way.

In a community, some laugh and some cry. It shouldn't always be the same people doing either one. Further, everyone shouldn't be expected to laugh or cry at the same time. We know that, but somehow, in the context of a congregation's work and worship, we have forgotten it. So let us remember, and then teach our children the importance of authenticity in worship rather than pretending.

Let us remember, and then teach our children, that we don't know, and will never know, all there is to know about God. We seem to have forgotten that God is God, beyond formula, definition, and lists of do's and don'ts. Let us teach our children that admitting there is more to God than we understand is not weakness on our part or aloofness on God's part. Rather, admitting that we don't know all there is to know about God is an act of submission to our Creator and King. It is the first step into the great mystery of God, a mystery that opens our hearts to growth rather than shrinking our hearts into indoctrination. We know, but have somehow forgotten along the way, that we should be suspicious of and watch out for those who claim to know all there is to know about God and who *question* the Christian faith of those who have *questions*.

Let us remember, and then teach our children, that Christian heritage and Christian tradition matter; that we didn't invent Christ-following or worship or church music. Let us remember, and then teach our children, that old paradigms are the foundation of what we do today, that tradition helps define us and gives us a story to take into the future.

In a time of racial profiling, suspicion, and fear, let us remember and then teach our children that "Jesus loves the little children of the world." Fear and hate will have to be overcome in order to accomplish this. Let us teach our children faith in God and confidence in the life and teachings of Jesus. Let us remember, and then teach our children, that the Bible is the sword of the Lord that pierces *our* hearts, not the sword of the self-righteousness that pierces only the hearts of the "bad guys."

Let us remember, and then teach our children, that forgiveness is a sign of strength, not a sign of weakness, that constraint is a sign of power. Let us teach our children to trust the truth of Jesus' upside down teachings.

In a time of terrorism and war, let us remember and then teach our children, that Jesus' love is "a fountain flowing deep and wide." It never stops flowing. It covers the whole earth. It covers *all* sin. "Deep and wide, deep and wide, there's a fountain flowing deep and wide" and that Jesus' teachings must be believed and his love lived. Let us remember, and then teach our children, that Jesus loves our enemies as much as he loves us.

In a time of unbridled consumption of resources, let us remember and then teach our children, that "this is our Father's world." Train their listening ears to the truth that "all nature sings and round us rings the music of the spheres." Let us remember, and then teach our children, to "rest in the thought of rocks and trees, of skies and seas," that it was "God's hand these wonders wrought," and that "all birds their carols raise" (even the eatable ones, and the ones whose nests get in the way of our expansion). Let us remember, and then teach our children, the importance of humility and moderation toward our planet and those with whom we inhabit this planet. Somehow, we have forgotten that much, maybe most, of what we are given, is given to us to share, not to consume. We have somehow forgotten, but let us remember and then teach our children that sharing is not only Christlike and biblical, it is an investment in our future. Individuals and nations don't hate us for sharing, they hate us for hoarding. They do not hate us for generosity, they hate us for greed. Sharing is a Christlike way of turning swords into plowshares.

Let us remember how, and then teach our children how, to learn from one another without being copycats. Let us remember the phrase our parents taught us, "I don't care if everyone else is doing it," and then let us teach that phrase to our children. This will keep them from following other churches into imported, and thus meaningless, worship styles. It will teach them to say "no" to political and social groundswells that get in the way of true Christ-following. It will teach them to say "yes" to thinking for themselves in the context of the life, work, and the teachings of Jesus. It will keep them in touch with the voice of their congregation. We know all this, but somehow, along the way, we've forgotten.

Let us remember, and then teach our children, that life's poetry is as important as life's prose, maybe more so. This is more than teaching our children that play is as important as work. It is teaching them to see poetry *in* their work and *in* the diversity of humanity and *in* the beauty of nature and *in* the mystery of God. There are too many people in our churches who see their relationship to God as one of God's policemen, pointing out who is thinking and acting out of line. There are too many people in our churches who are invigorated only by what they are against. There is no poetry in their lives, only the prose of lists and labels: lists of what to do and what not to do, lists of who is right and who is wrong, lists of what sins are acceptable and what sins are not, labels that signify the other person's deficiency. There are too many people in our churches who are afraid of the Bible's poetry, focusing only on its prose, as they interpret it in the context of their own agendas. God spare our children from a life of seeing the Bible and their faith as nothing more than a list of rules and a theology of works.

Let us remember, and then teach our children, while they still know how to play, that Sabbath is not sloth, but is, in fact, an act of obedience. We are not called to produce results in worship. Therefore, we need not deny the voice of our congregation in order to accomplish something. Let us remember and then teach our children that being a workaholic not only fails to impress God, it is a form of idolatry; giving God's time to someone or something else. We know that, we've simply forgotten it along the way. Perhaps this thought is best expressed by saying we should let our children teach us about play, and imagination, and the need for naps (Sabbath).

Along those same lines, let us remember and then teach our children that silence is not something they should fear, rather it is a place to find themselves and God. Silence is a place to come clean with God. Let us teach them that coming clean before God is a momentous project. Let us teach our children to cherish silence when they bump into it and to create it when none is to be found.

Let us remember, and then teach our children, that the cross of Christ was not and is not painted red, white, and blue; that there is a difference between being a Christian and being an

American, that patriotism and discipleship are not synonymous, that while we stand when we hear the National Anthem, we bow when we hear the voice of God. The voice of the congregation is to be in prayerful dialogue with the voice of God; silent after voicing prayer to hear the voice of God.

Let us remember that these precious young lives are not meant to be our clones, carrying on our agendas. Rather, they belong to Jesus and we are to help them open their hearts toward Christlikeness, even if their Spirit-led life paths don't lead them toward the money, popularity, and comfort we would wish for them. Let us teach them that they are not to mimic another congregation's voice in an attempt to make their worship profitable.

What shall we teach our children? The question causes us to examine our own Christ-following and worship in the deepest recesses of our own hearts. For, if we are to be authentic worshipers and disciples, we must teach from that depth. We will find ourselves teaching ourselves while we teach our children. There is nothing more frightening than a teacher who has ceased to be a learner, unless it is a messenger who has forgotten his or her voice, or a worshiping congregation that is pretending to be what they are not.

What shall we teach our children? Let us teach them what we used to know, but have somehow forgotten.

Dear God, let the things we shall teach our children bring us to our knees and to tears, crying for mercy and singing your praise in the authentic voice of our congregation. In Jesus' name, Amen.

God bless you as you seek to discover, recover, trust, share the good news in, and worship authentically in the voice of your congregation.